The
Presence
The Ministry of the Holy Spirit

Arnold Prater

OLIVER
NELSON

THOMAS NELSON PUBLISHERS
Nashville

Published in Nashville, Tennessee, by Oliver-Nelson Books, a division of Thomas Nelson, Inc., Publishers, and distributed in Canada by Word Communications, Ltd., Richmond, British Columbia, and in the United Kingdom by Word (UK), Ltd., Milton Keynes, England.

Library of Congress Cataloging-in-Publication Data

Prater, Arnold.
    The presence / Arnold Prater.
        p.   cm.
    ISBN 0-8407-9676-5 (pbk.)
    1. Holy Spirit.   2. Fruit of the Spirit.   I. Title.
BT121.2.P73   1993
231'.3—dc20   93–4502
                                                                        CIP

Printed in the United States of America.
1 2 3 4 5 6 — 98 97 96 95 94 93

CONTENTS

INTRODUCTION

Someone Out There Keeps Following Me Around

Stop and think a minute. Do you remember when, as a child, you became aware of silence for the first time—when for the first time you really *heard* it? You stood and listened, and it was there, so loud and persistent it almost rang.

Perhaps it was at night, and you were lying in bed. Or you were in a forest or a cave. Because you were alone, you became aware of it. It was big and round, extending in every direction.

You could not escape the silence. You could look up, walk a few steps, or lie flat on your back; but when you listened from any position, it was still there.

The other night I was in the yard listening to the song of a mockingbird. Its melodies were stabbing the darkness with sharp, laser-beam-like staccato notes. Suddenly the singing stopped, and the silence crashed in on my eardrums like the ring of a hammer striking an anvil.

Have you had it happen to you? The only way you can escape it is to speak, cry out, or run to a place where people are laughing and talking.

Someone keeps following me around who is like the silence. He surrounds me completely. No matter where I go or what I do, that Someone is right there.

When I awaken in the morning, He is there. I am only vaguely aware of His presence during the day while I am busy with the things I must do, such as going to the cleaners or fixing the bathroom faucet or working at my word processor.

Each day is like a series of paragraphs. As I perform each task, little indentions appear in the margin, little pauses as I move from situation to situation—times when I am alone driving to the supermarket, when I walk into the backyard to fix the sprinkler, or when I go into the kitchen for a cup of coffee. Into these paragraph-like indentions of the day the awareness of His presence comes rushing like a bag of tightly bound beads, suddenly broken and spilling everywhere until I am quickly surrounded and flooded again with the sense of it.

I received Jesus Christ as my Lord and Savior at the age of ten. But they taught me in Sunday school that He was seated at the right hand of the Father. So who was this Someone who kept following me around?

Far into my adult years I was still asking the question. I was like Jacob, wrestling in the midnight with a stranger. Finally, there came a pause in their struggle. Jacob, panting from exertion, whispered hoarsely, "Tell me Your name, I pray." The Lord answered, "Why is it that you ask about My name?" (Gen. 32:29). He did not satisfy Jacob with an answer.

So for years I did not know His name. Oh, it passed my lips many times, but it did not issue forth from my heart.

Then came that life-changing time when that

One, that Presence around me, entered my being and filled me. Now there was no way one could draw lines and say, "This is inside, and this is out."

It was in that experience of "entering in" that I finally discovered the name of that Someone who had been following me around all of my life, the One who had been wooing and waiting to make me His own, who had now consummated our oneness with a great infilling of Himself.

His name was *Holy*. Ever since, I have known Him as the Holy Spirit, the Holy Ghost, the Holy Guest, or simply the Presence.

Of course, I had known Him *intellectually*. I had known Him in the same sense that I knew the queen of England. I knew that He *was*, but now I knew Him personally. I knew that He *is*.

At this point, like every illustration that seeks to describe God, the metaphor of the silence breaks down. If you spend your life trying to define God, you will never know Him.

I cannot define the Holy Spirit, but I can say this: He is the One who puts the pizzazz, the glory, the carbonation, the fizz into life—things that, for the Christian, make the difference between pointless existence and real living.

FOR

That great army of God's people who are mature enough that though they may disagree at various points of doctrine, still find the grace to be one with each other in Christian love and in exalting Jesus.

Glory!

Chapter 1

The Here-and-Now God

His fighter plane badly damaged, he is returning to his base in Saudi Arabia. While on a mission to Baghdad, his plane has caught some antiaircraft shrapnel.

He is nearing home, but he has a big problem. It is night, and a thick fog has formed. There is no way he can see even the lights of the runway, much less the runway. As the plane quickly loses power, he knows he has only one chance to land.

He is encouraged by the voice in his headset. "No need to bail out! Just listen to us, and we'll bring you in," it says. But he is receiving a second set of signals from his senses telling him the nose of his plane is slanting downward at a dangerous angle and his right wing is dropping. Everything in him tells him, "Lift your nose! Lift that wing! You are swinging too far to the right! Correct! Correct!"

Still, the voice in his headset assures him, "You're doing great. That's perfect. Hold it right there!"

So here is the life-or-death question: *Which voice are you going to believe?* Will you believe your senses, which depend only on your knowledge from tasting, touching, hearing, feeling, and seeing? Or will you believe the other voice, which has access to infinitely more reliable and accurate information?

Herein lies the dilemma of those who would turn every area of their lives over to the here-and-now God. On one hand, when critical decisions or learning situations arise, it is easy to believe what our minds tell us, either from one or more of the five senses or from human logic and reasoning. Or should we believe the inner Voice, the Holy Spirit, who Jesus said would "guide you into all truth" (John 16:13)? It is so much easier simply to read our devotional booklets in the morning, say a little prayer, go to worship on Sunday, then on Monday lose ourselves in the great stream of the world.

A little girl was helping her mother put away the Christmas decorations. She took the crèche with the manger and the Baby lying in it, closed the lid on the box, and said, "There, Mother, we can put Jesus away for another year!"

Many people are like that. After doing the usual things on Sunday, they put Him away for another week.

The great cosmic Father we can accept. The risen Jesus we can acknowledge. But the idea of deep, personal intimacy with the living God, who loves us so much that He is not satisfied to be trapped in a concept or locked in the pages of a Holy Book, is very difficult for us to receive.

We can believe in Him as a nearby God while we are alone in our closets, but it is especially difficult for us to relate Him to everyday life. What has God to do with crowded freeways where wild drivers make obscene gestures at us and cut across four lanes, barely missing us? Does He care about office feuds and crabby bosses? Can He relate to grumpy husbands, crying babies, and supermarket carts with wobbly or frozen wheels?

Yet these are the situations in which the Holy Presence works the very best! But it is so hard for us to relate the Father we worship on Sunday in such stained-glass pomp, majesty, and glory to all that happens in this secular madhouse!

I really don't know why, unless it is because we know that if we get too intimate with the living

Presence, He might make some demands on us that we don't want to hear.

But something about that answer doesn't satisfy me. Could it be that we have a deep uneasiness about letting Someone we can't see or hear take charge of everything—our time, talents, businesses, families—*everything*?

Perhaps that is partly true, but I really believe we leave God out of our everyday experiences because we have neglected the doctrine of the Holy Spirit to the point that two or three generations have grown up without being taught the beauty and the power of His very personal Presence. Or perhaps what little teaching we received was couched in terms so theologically obtuse that we average folks did not understand and lost interest.

My father was a pastor who devoted his entire ministry to preaching from the evangelical point of view. He was filled with the Spirit of God, but he never taught or preached very much about the Holy Spirit. It was not because he was not interested. I suspect it was because the denomination as a whole ignored the subject in his generation.

Now all of that has changed. In the sixties the Spirit of God decided it was time to widen His activities to the masses. So He chose to break into the mainstream of believers in the most unlikely place of all, the Roman Catholic church. Next, being totally beyond human predictability, He broke into the second most unlikely place, the Episcopal church. From there He went raging through all the denominations until now the stream of the Holy Spirit, the here-and-now God, is rolling along at flood tide.

To bypass the Holy Spirit (God with us and in us)

is to shatter the true nature of the Trinity. Without God here and now in everyday, heavy-traffic, grocery-shopping, meat-and-potato situations makes of the Father simply a coach standing on the sidelines, sending in instructions but never actually getting into the game Himself. That concept negates at least half of all Jesus taught. It also ignores the life drive of spiritual giants of the past whose compassion for souls and the downtrodden was basic to their understanding of the gospel.

Without a biscuit-and-gravy, Monday-morning type of relationship the Holy Spirit truly becomes a holy "ghost," a wispy, mysterious something, dutifully keeping out of sight most of the time, as all good ghosts do. He appears just before bedtime and at the breakfast table when we say a prayer over our food and acknowledge that there is a Supreme Being. Otherwise, He is safely kept between the pages of our Bibles so He can't get out into the world where we live our lives. The Holy Presence, then, becomes a little vest-pocket God whom we can tuck away during the week and bring out on Sunday morning, then put Him away to rest until the next Sunday, until Uncle John is taken to the intensive-care unit, or until the baby gets sick.

That concept is aeons away from the Spirit who came roaring into the lives of the disciples at pentecost like a jet breaking the sound barrier, who is real and breathtakingly alive in this world today! The fact remains that the Father's promise has been fulfilled, and many have reaped the harvest of an abundant life as benefactors of that promise. John Wesley's last words gave an elegant testimony to that fact: "The best of all is, God is with us."

My purpose in these pages is to present an understanding of what the blessed Spirit should mean in our lives from an everyday, here-and-now viewpoint. If fellowship in and with the Spirit is not real where we live our lives each day, then He doesn't really matter. But if He is real and truly is our life guide, *nothing else* finally matters!

I want to express the glory and the wonder of this majestic and almost incomprehensible truth in plain, down-from-glory, up-from-earth English so all who are truly seeking may be blessed and may be filled with the indwelling "fullness of God" (Eph. 3:19). Too many people and local churches have waited too long to shed their fears and come face-to-face with Him in the taut, stress-filled streets of everyday living, where the acids of sin run raw in the gutters of life.

At the heart of almost every local church is a small band of people who are gloriously dedicated and excited about their walk with the Lord. Any pastor would tell you, "I don't know what I'd do without them!" But I believe, standing on the sidelines, are thousands of sincere people who would like to go deeper into the grace and knowledge of God but don't know how because they have never been taught.

It is highly significant that after God, through Jeremiah, promised the coming of the Spirit, it was six hundred years before it came to pass! As the old proverb states, God may not always show up when you thought He would, but He will always be on time!

Perhaps you've been waiting a long time to know Him in a far more intimate and personal way than ever before. Perhaps that time has come!

Chapter 2

An Announcement That Wasn't in the Bulletin

It was a hot August day. A man sat on the curb of a well that was the water supply for the nearby village. He had been walking since daylight, and He was tired and thirsty.

A woman walked through the village gate balancing a water pot on her head. Since it was only noon and the hour for the village women to come for water was 4:00 P.M., the man knew she was an outcast. But He said a perfectly natural thing to her: "Give Me a drink" (John 4:7). The woman was so shocked that she almost dropped her water pot. She asked Him, "Why do you even speak to me, much less ask for water? Don't you know, first, I am a woman and second, I am a Samaritan?" (John 4:9, paraphrased).

Not wanting to dignify that question with an answer, Jesus ignored it and said, "If you knew the gift of God, and who it is who says to you, 'Give Me a drink,' you would have asked Him, and He would have given you living water" (John 4:10).

"If you knew the gift of God . . ." What was it?

Jesus was a man with a burning secret. On the inside He was bursting with the good news of that secret. But He was not yet at liberty to tell it to His people! However, He was so full of it that He could not keep it all to Himself, so in this charming incident He let out a bit of the news. (Please read the account in John 4 to refresh your memory.)

This woman was the first person mentioned in the New Testament to whom Jesus revealed His true identity: "I who speak to you am He [the Messiah]" (John 4:26).

Jesus also revealed to her the mercy and compassion of the One who was to come as the Holy Spirit, for in verse 21 He called her "woman." The Greek word *gune,* which is used here, is not used for scolding or contempt but is used lovingly as a term of great endearment. At a Bible conference I heard a teacher say that the term meant "special lady." Think of it: this woman is a village outcast, cannot associate with the other women, has been divorced several times, and is now living with a man who is not her husband. Yet Jesus, seeing the possibilities in her, calls her "special lady"! He used the same word for this woman that He used for His mother at the wedding in Cana and on the cross.

It is no wonder that at Jacob's well He said, "If you knew the gift of God, and who it is who says to you, 'Give Me a drink,' you would have asked Him, and He would have given you living water" (John 4:10). With this secret locked in His heart He said, in effect, with a yearning she could never understand, "Oh, if only I could tell you about the gift the Father is going to give!"

When Jesus Broke Up the Service

Jesus went to the Feast of Tabernacles (also called Booths), which every Jewish male living within twenty-one miles of Jerusalem was required to attend. On the last great day of the joyous festival, which included much dancing, singing of psalms, and thanksgiving for the blessings of God, came a moment of respectful and reverent silence. At that moment the priest, who had gone down to the pool of Siloam to draw a golden pitcher of water, came back into the courtyard of the temple, where the ornate altar had been constructed. At its corners four golden oil lamps burned brightly. The priest ascended a ladder, for the altar was quite high, and poured the pitcher of water on the altar, signifying thanksgiving for God's gift of water in an arid and parched land where water was (and still is) a treasure.

This was the highest, climactic moment of the festival. Just as the priest poured the water, the stillness was shattered by the sound of Jesus' strong voice. It pierced the assembly like a gunshot ringing in startling staccato off a canyon wall, demanding attention. He simply *had* to let it go. He could contain the secret no longer.

John said He "cried out, saying, 'If anyone thirsts, let him come to Me and drink. He who believes in Me, as the Scripture has said, out of his heart will flow rivers of living water'" (John 7:37–38). Translations vary here. Some say He "stood up and proclaimed." Others use words such as *exclaimed* and *shouted*; but in any event He let it all out! He shouted!

Then the Gospel says, "But this He spoke concerning the Spirit, whom those believing in Him would receive; for the Holy Spirit was not yet given, because Jesus was not yet glorified [had not yet finished His work]" (v. 39).

I imagine that almost broke up the service. What would happen in your church one Sunday morning if someone suddenly stood up at the most crucial point in the worship and issued a proclamation? To say the least, it would certainly knock a hole in the order of worship, confuse the ushers, wake up the sleeping, shake up the pastor, and grab the whole-hearted attention of the congregation in an instant!

Jesus, being human as well as divine, had trouble keeping a secret. Most people have the same problem, especially if they know it is going to bring joy and delight to someone they love.

Once my wife, Miss Martha, lost her wedding ring. It simply disappeared. Whether it went down the drain, fell off the cabinet, or was laid somewhere and forgotten, we never knew. At any rate, it was gone.

It was a very cheap ring. I had bought it when we were very, very poor, and I made payments on it for months and months. I thought I would never finish the payments. In fact, I think that is when I first began to believe in eternal life!

The years passed, and I kept thinking someday she would find the ring. I finally decided that was not going to happen, so I bought a ring and planned to give it to her for Christmas. It was much more expensive and more beautiful than the original.

We decorated the tree, and I wrapped the ring in a big box to confuse her. She tried to guess what was in it. Day after day she shook and rattled that box.

Meanwhile, I stood by, almost bursting with excitement and joy because I knew how thrilled and excited she was going to be. My love for her only intensified my joy and made the secret more difficult to keep.

When the great day came and she opened the box and beheld her new ring, she was so overjoyed that I lived on my brownie points for days!

I believe something like this was going on inside Jesus at Jacob's well and at the Feast of Tabernacles. It is the nature of love to be excited at the prospect of bringing joy and fulfillment to the beloved. He knew the gift that was to come.

Plain Talk from the Master

Jesus said no more about His secret until the Cross drew very near. Then in the last week of His life He let out the secret. He told all. But He was like a college professor trying to explain calculus to a class of first graders. It was like throwing popcorn at the Grand Coulee Dam. The news bounced off them. They simply could not comprehend it.

He began by trying to lay the groundwork for their comprehension of the Trinity. In John 14 Philip said, "Show us the Father, and it is sufficient for us" (v. 8). Then Jesus dropped this blockbuster on them: "He who has seen Me has seen the Father" (v. 9)!

No sane mortal could have ever said that. But that was not all. He said, "I will ask the Father, and He will send another Helper, the Spirit of truth" (vv. 16–17, paraphrased). Then He said something even more mysterious: "He dwells with you and will be in you" (v. 17).

They could not comprehend it then, but on the other side of pentecost they knew, and they knew for certain. What He had meant was, "I *must* go away, for as long as I walk among you, I am separated from you by time and geography and space. And that's too limiting; it's too far from you. But when I come back again in the Holy Spirit, I will dwell *in* you." Thus, Jesus described an intimacy which, at that point, they could scarcely imagine.

Then He gave them more plain talk that perhaps they understood a little better: "When the Holy Spirit comes, His job in you will be to teach you truth you need to know as you are able to comprehend it and to enable you to recall supernaturally the things I have taught you" (v. 26, paraphrased).

"But that's not all! There's more. When the Spirit of truth comes, He will convict the world of its sin and make it aware of the God who from His kindness and grace waits to forgive it" (John 16:8, paraphrased).

Then He concluded, "When the Holy Spirit dwells in you, He will not allow you to exalt Him, for His job will be to exalt Me and to lift Me up to the world" (John 16:13-14, paraphrased).

All of that (and more) is contained in John 14—16. Take time now to read those chapters and meditate on them. If the majesty and magnificent truth of these revelations really hits you, you may find yourself having a spasm of sheer joy at the Father's graciousness and great love for you!

The disciples became totally aware of all this only after pentecost. I can identify with their rush of joy from their sudden insight and understanding. Sometimes truth has come upon me in that manner.

When I was in the fourth grade, I had some subjects in which I was pretty good and some in which I was only fair, but I had one in which I was, well, horrible. That was math. All those numbers looked to me like spaghetti that had suddenly been dumped from a can, and I was required to pick out the single strands and weave them into a sensible pattern. No matter how I racked my brain, it was all an insanely whirling mass of gobbledygook! My teacher was a very loving, compassionate woman who knew I was struggling. So she took extra time with me and was very patient as she explained things.

One glorious day I saw it! All the spaghetti started

making sense. After I made the first discovery, more understanding came gushing down like rainwater from a downspout. In two weeks I had caught up with the rest of the class.

Recognizing truth is a process that almost always comes slowly, like watching a golden harvest moon in October rise and gradually throw its orange light across the celebrating hillsides. But sometimes truth explodes within you and pierces you like a star shell, lighting up the countryside of your mind with the brilliant light of sudden understanding.

At pentecost the harvest moon rose, the star shell exploded, and all the spaghetti came unscrambled. Let's hurry on and see what happened!

Chapter 3

When the Tornado Came Unharnessed

I remember once as a very small child, on a very hot summer day, blissfully riding my tricycle down the sidewalk about a block from our house. I was very much intent on the things in my little world: the lines dividing sections of the concrete, leaves that crackled under my wheels, a parade of ants that I rudely invaded.

Suddenly there was a tremendous flash of lightning, followed by a cannonade of thunder, which was followed immediately by tremendous, blinding sheets of rain.

As my little legs frantically pumped the tricycle homeward, I was literally yanked out of the safety of my own little world of childhood fantasies into the reality of a completely new and utterly awesome dimension. In no way could I ever have dreamed beforehand that such an experience could bring about a complete change of perspective and could do so almost instantly.

Something like this happened at pentecost.

The Tornado Comes Unharnessed

They had been astounded by the resurrection. Dead people just don't come back to life, but this one did! They saw Him; they heard Him; they touched Him. John later was to say, "That which was from the beginning, which we have heard, which we have seen with our eyes, which we have looked upon, and *our hands have handled*" (1 John 1:1, italics added). John was expressing awe about a man who was obviously dead when they took Him down from the cross—eyes rolled back, a slight stiffening of the joints, cyanosis of the lips. *That* man they now had seen alive and never more dynamically filled with divine energy. His body had been new and glorified. Then they had watched with open mouths as He was miraculously taken up into heaven in a cloud.

All this occurred after He had told them to wait a while, and the promise of the Father, the coming of the Spirit of truth, which was to be *in* them, would be made manifest *among* them. So they had gathered in the room where they commonly met each day and waited, 120 of them, including the eleven disciples. Among the number were Mary, the mother of Jesus, and His brothers. They were discussing some of the strange things the Master had said, which they did not understand, trying to unravel the mystery of how a dead man could come back to life, marveling that in the wonderful chemistry of God sometimes nothing succeeds like failure. Day after day they had gathered here, trying to unravel the mystery of God's plan for His church.

Suddenly it happened—not from the southwest or the northeast but from heaven. From above there descended on these resurrection witnesses a mighty, tornadic wind that shook the building and roared so they could not hear one another speak. As if that were not enough, "divided tongues, as of fire" (Acts 2:3) appeared, one over the head of each of them, and we might speculate that the flames smelled of ozone, similar to that which lingers after lightning strikes nearby.

As the sound of the wind began to die, one by one they arose from their shock and began to speak, not in Aramaic but with strange sounds they later learned were foreign tongues they had not learned.

As they went into the streets, propelled by this

phenomenal but strangely sweet and fulfilling occurrence, strangers from other lands gathered and heard them tell the great works of God in their native tongues. The Spirit had come and had filled them to overflowing.

Why No Mighty Winds or Tongues as of Fire Today?

When God wants to get our attention, He knows full well how to do it. Three things always get the job done: earthquakes, storms, and fire.

At pentecost God used all three of these headline makers. The storm (wind) and fire came at pentecost, and in almost an instant replay a short time later He gave an earthquake. They had prayed, and the building began to shake, "and they were all filled with the Holy Spirit and began to speak with other tongues, as the Spirit gave them utterance" (Acts 2:4; see also Acts 4:31).

Some deny the reality of the infilling of the Holy Spirit in today's world by asking, "If this really happens today, where are the mighty winds and the tongues as of fire?" The Father knew that only the spectacular would get people's attention. It took the crucifixion and the resurrection to make them realize that Jesus Christ was who He said He was. Two pretty spectacular events, I'm sure you will agree. But now He had a further revelation for them. This was a kindergarten experience for all of them, the first stages of their education, so to speak. So He provided the mighty wind and the tongues as of fire.

Still, people with honest doubts legitimately ask, "If experiencing the infilling of the Holy Spirit is real, where are these signs today?" We once had the great privilege of having E. Stanley Jones preach for a week in our church. Someone asked him this question, and he replied, "The wind and the tongues as of fire were scaffolding, needed to erect the building; but once the structure was in place, they were no longer needed and could be taken away." After that they had to be replaced by faith. From then on, once their attention and perception had been gained, the disciples and all the generations since are asked to walk by faith and to receive the Holy Spirit by virtue of what the Word of God promises.

The Bible says that "without faith it is impossible to please Him" (Heb. 11:6). You may be assured that no matter by what route God is leading us, we will come to a chasm called faith. At that chasm personal knowledge ceases, and the only way across it is by a leap of faith. A friend of mine says, "Understanding can wait; obedience cannot."

It is on the other side of that chasm that understanding awaits.

God in Three Acts

I love a good play, live and on stage, performed by actors who really get into their parts.

The one I love best is the most amazing, fascinating drama conceivable, the one being played on the stage of human history. While watching and studying that drama the other day, I discovered something so exciting and awesome that I could hardly wait to share it.

In the Beginning

If you read the Bible straight through, you discover that God revealed Himself gradually to His people as they grew and matured and became capable of receiving what He wanted to show them about Himself.

In act 1 God revealed Himself as Father-Creator. He created the heavens and the earth, and everything was perfect until his two human creatures used their free choice to mess it up.

In the beginning there were only peace and harmony between the Creator and the created. But then the plot thickened. The snake hissed, and sin entered from downstage. Between a holy, sinless God and sinful, imperfect humanity a great gulf was created.

Since He is a loving being, God wanted to bridge that gulf, for love like God's is never satisfied apart from the beloved. So He searched the earth and found a people who had only one God. He called the Israelites and made a covenant with them through Abraham, promising that He would be their God and that they would be His people.

Gradually, as they began to grow spiritually, He began to show them a little more of Himself. They saw Him first as the great cosmic Creator, holy but very distant. He was greatly to be feared. They would not even speak His name for fear of retribution for their irreverence.

Then they began to see Him as a national God, the God who delivered their nation from Egypt and went before them as a pillar of cloud by day and a pillar of fire by night. This God lived on the stormy heights of a smoking mountain called Sinai. Sometimes when He was angry, the lightning came, the thunder rolled, and the earth trembled. When He was pleased, the crops were good, pastures were lush, and the land yielded abundance.

One day this God who lived on the mountain sent them a love note saying, "If you want to find happiness, this is the way." The law came on stone tablets; but as time went by, they found that the law was too much for them. They couldn't live up to it. They found that they were living under guilt and condemnation, so they came to see God as a kind of sky-snoop who peered around the corners, peeping into their lives.

With the law came sin-consciousness, so they established rites and rituals and sacrifices to try and make atonement, to bring their nation to "at-oneness" with Him. Their priests devised a system of animal sacrifices to try and make atonement for their disobedience. Later, their prophets warned them that God was not pleased with their rites and rituals and prophesied that the day would come when a Messiah would become the sacrifice. If they believed in Him, their sins could be forgiven.

Now it was time to move past ceremonies and rituals. It was time for the second act.

The Second Act Begins

"When the fullness of the time had come, God sent forth His Son" (Gal. 4:4). At just the right time God Himself answered their cry for help and became a human being in Jesus Christ. A few people came to believe in Him, though many refused to be rescued from the swamp of self-sufficiency. He came down to earth to reveal Himself as a one-to-one God and as One whose very name, Jesus, meant "Savior from sin."

Those who believed came to see that God was not the wrathful, angry One who lived on the mountain, the Creator God who was spying on them, who issued prosperity certificates of deposit to the righteous and filed bankruptcy claims against the wicked. Rather, God was like Jesus Christ.

They saw Him walk among them, healing the sick. They watched Him love tax collectors and fishers. They saw Him forgive harlots and thieves. Finally, they saw Him dragged out to a little mountain shaped like death itself and watched Him die because of what they were.

Tragedy had torn a gaping hole in their expectations, and they ran away in fear and disappointment. But then He blasted the door off the tomb of Joseph of Arimathea and appeared to them, and Thomas fell at His feet and spoke for the rest of them—and for all today who need forgiveness, love, and a way out—when he cried, "My Lord and my God!" (John 20:28). They found that when they claimed Him as Savior, their burdens were lifted; the guilt was gone.

Then finally, a few weeks later, they watched as the pull of heaven became stronger than the pull of earth, and He ascended into it and sat down at the right hand of the ultimate Authority.

When He did that, He blew the roof off human despair!

Coincidence or Plan?

I have already described the third act. It happened when the "tornado" came unharnessed at pentecost. The disciples were filled with the Holy Spirit, which the Father, through Joel and others through the centuries, had promised to send. The Holy Spirit was poured out on "all flesh," on all who would receive Him.

Now let me share with you the discovery I made that is tremendously exciting to me in this three-act drama we have been watching together. One day while thinking about God's gradual revelation of Himself to humanity, I came to this sudden, thrilling realization: *that God has chosen to reveal Himself to individual persons in precisely the same way by which He has revealed Himself to humanity in the Scriptures!* He is still using the three-act method today!

I daresay He has revealed Himself to you as He has to me, first as the great Creator-God. When you were a child, your first image of God was a sort of ominous, "Big Daddy" in the sky. He made everything; He knew everything; and He was pleased when you did right and punished you when you did wrong.

In Sunday school they taught me that God is like a Father. To tell the truth, that made me somewhat afraid of Him. My father was head of the "swat team" around our house. He would swat me on the generous fatty tissue of my backside, where it would tickle my remembrance the most! So in spite of everything, God remained the "Big Man" who lived far off in the sky.

True, you said your childhood prayers.

> God is great, God is good,
> Now we thank Him for our food.

If you went to Sunday school, you probably brought home leaflets depicting the Good Shepherd. But in spite of all this, when you heard about turning the Nile into blood and rolling back the massive waters of the Red Sea and some of the early kings and their terrible wars, there lurking in the back of your mind was the picture of God as a father figure all right, but He was pretty ominous, and you had better watch out!

In your junior-high days you became sin-conscious. You knew the meaning of disobedience and some of the consequences it brought because you had disobeyed and had been punished. Like Israel of old, almost unconsciously there grew in you a deep need for forgiveness and acceptance. You needed a Savior.

The first act was over. The second act began, and you began to seek for yourself. Finally, you found Him. Perhaps it was in a confirmation class or at the altar in a series of meetings or in the privacy of your room. No matter where you found Him, faith rose within you, and you admitted Him into your heart as Savior. The load was lifted; the guilt was gone. Your name was written in the Lamb's Book of Life.

You would still have to be forgiven time and time again along the way, but God became the great Accepter, the great Forgiver, the great Lover of your soul. Act 2 was completed in you.

That, more or less, is the way it happens to those who call ourselves Christian disciples. It is surely no coincidence that the biblical and personal revelations of God to us are identical. That is His plan.

But for many, the third act, pentecost, has not yet happened.

Why Fear the Holy Spirit?

Natives of the Ozark hills sometimes use the expression "We'uns are down on what we ain't up on!" We fear the unknown.

Most of us who have come from traditional churches love Christmas! Christmas is a joy to us, and we know how to celebrate it! We change the paraments to Advent purple, and we mount the Advent wreath with its five candles and purple ribbon.

We celebrate the hanging of the green; we practice the Christmas tableaux with our little children; and we frantically make angels' wings, shepherds' robes, and costumes for the wise men.

Then comes the Sunday night before Christmas and the children's program. Better come early if you want a good seat in the balcony. And don't forget to bring your camcorder.

Then comes Christmas Eve Communion, and everyone lights a candle and processes from the sanctuary. I tell you, Christmas in the traditional church is very special!

Do we ever love Easter! In fact, we begin celebrating on Ash Wednesday, when Lent begins. Special services are held, leading to the Maundy-evening holy Communion or a Tenebrae (candlelighting) service.

Then comes the somber Good Friday afternoon service, perhaps a community affair, and maybe a glorious cantata that night.

Finally, Easter morning comes. There is a sunrise

service, followed by great worship services of celebration, and we rise in our packed sanctuaries to sing, "Up from the grave He arose."

Oh, how we love Christmas and Easter! And why? They are both structured for us. They are predictable! We can control them. We know how everything is going to come out! Therefore, they do not threaten us. At Christmas we know that there will be shepherds, angel choruses, and wise men. There will be a crèche with the Baby in it and Joseph and Mary and the animals. At Easter we know that Jesus is going to be betrayed and crucified. We know that Peter will deny Him, that the disciples will run away, and that Mary will go to the tomb early in the morning and meet the Lord.

We love it because we know what is going to happen, for it's all laid out for us. It's beautiful but not risky, because neither Christmas nor Easter will ever upset our traditional celebrations, nor should they.

But pentecost! Ah yes, pentecost. Well, that's a different story.

Oh, we give it a rather polite nod. We put on red paraments, and if we use bulletins, they are decorated with fiery red emblems. But truthfully, we are just a bit relieved when it is all over and we can return to the routine for another year.

Why are we, who come from traditional fellowships, so afraid of pentecost? It just might be because pentecost is not organized in advance. It is not neatly laid out for us. The narrative simply does not lend itself to drama and tableaux.

Pentecost is unpredictable. If we turn the Holy Spirit loose, He just might do something that is not in the bulletin, and that might shake up many of us!

Who can put a harness on a tornado? What kind of chemical do you use to control a spiritual fire? "Where the Spirit of the Lord is, there is liberty," says the Bible (2 Cor. 3:17), not just liberty for the people but also liberty for the Holy Spirit Himself!

Once a minister was stopped by a curious policeman who had seen the clergy sticker on the bumper of his car. He asked, "Reverend, I've been wanting to know for a long time, what does 'D.D.' after a minister's name mean?"

The minister replied, "It stands for 'doctor of divinity'!" The policeman replied, "Wow! Does that ever relieve me! On the police blotter it means 'drunk and disorderly'!"

Let me make two things clear. First, I am not calling for disorderliness in churches. Second, I am simply calling for freedom for the Spirit to do what He pleases.

I have not taken my word processor in hand to bash traditional churches. Far from it. They do not deserve that from me. And besides, they have always been more than gracious to me, and I love them. But Miss Martha is not perfect either, and you'll never know how much I love her! Whoever waits for perfection in people or denominations to begin loving will never do it. However, it is my conviction that one of the great spiritual root causes of declining membership in traditional churches has been our sheer neglect of sound teaching about who the Holy Spirit is and what He proposes to do in our lives.

Most comfortable church members I know have left the play at the end of the second act, either thinking it was concluded or fearing to face the third. When we stop at the resurrection and do not go on to pentecost, we fragment the orderliness of the Godhead (Trinity), and God fractionalized is less than God. Our dear pentecostal and holiness brothers and sisters know that. When God is prohibited from playing out the drama of revelation He has planned for each of us, the result is that it sometimes produces either carnal Christians or those who are lukewarm, and both are anathema to the Father.

One purpose of this book is to call the church's ministers, leaders, and teachers to begin an informed and balanced program of emphasis and teaching on the work and person of the Holy Spirit and to ask His forgiveness for neglecting Him. At the same time, I hope to help the body of Christ understand who God has revealed Himself to be and what He desires from us. The only way I know to do that is to write as honestly as I can about what has been revealed to me through the Scriptures and through personal experiences along the way.

It is sad to have to say this because we should already know it, but the church has nothing to fear from the Holy Spirit, and neither do we as individuals. God will never ask us to do something outside the context of our own personhood, for when He formed us in our mother's womb, He gave each of us a uniqueness. That uniqueness is precious to Him. He programmed us with possibilities that would leave us breathless if we could see where they would finally lead us if we allowed them.

But the problem may be with the preconceptions we have carried all our lives as to just how deep and how far that personhood of ours can grow and be stretched. Most people measure themselves by their limitations instead of by their possibilities.

My father as a youth was an uneducated, rather wild, rebellious, sometimes crude person living in the rugged and undeveloped Ozark mountains of southwest Missouri. But in Christ after forty-six years in the ministry he rose to be one of the most respected ministers in the denomination, gaining many honors and gathering a fantastic amount of fruit for the kingdom.

Following his retirement, I sat on his front porch and asked, "Father, what is the one thing you know about God today that you didn't know when you began your ministry?"

Without hesitation he answered, *"That there is no limit to what God can do with a life that is totally given to Him!"*

Here is a rough, uneducated, coarse, blunt man named Peter, the hard crust of whose being had been baked in the hot suns of the Sea of Galilee. Suddenly this man, who was never before noted for his courage, stands up after the Holy Spirit has filled him at pentecost and preaches elegantly for one hour, and three thousand people fall to their knees crying out for God!

If you had been there and had known Peter all his life, you might have gone up to him and said in astonishment, "Why Peter, I never knew you had that in you!" And I daresay Peter would have replied with a hearty laugh, "Well, bless the Lord, neither did I!"

Let me say again that God will never embarrass us or ask us to do something that is foreign to the way He made us; but if He had perfect freedom in our lives to perfect that which He began, He just might expand our personhood, illuminate it, and impart to it new and exciting dimensions we never dreamed possible!

The truth is that the great Father-Creator-God of whom we were so afraid as children lives in us to love us with a love the depths of which we can never fully probe here. He wants nothing but the very best for each one of us. We need to face it: as adults, *if we are afraid of the Holy Spirit, we are afraid of God!* I wonder if He doesn't sometimes become very sorrowful because we use our free choice to shackle and limit Him.

A popular chorus goes, "O how He loves you and me!" If only we could let ourselves believe that!

It is reported that Archimedes once said that if he had a lever to place under the world and if it were long enough, he could sit on the end of it and lift the world. God has loved us enough that at pentecost He has lifted the world; but instead of a lever, He sent a Lover!

But before we can turn that Lover loose in our lives, we must answer more fully the question we raised in the beginning, "Just who is this Someone who keeps following us around?"

Chapter 4

Who Is This Ghost Called Holy?

Suppose someone knocked at your door one night and asked if he could come in and live with you the rest of your life. That is not very likely to happen; but if it did, I imagine the first question you would ask would be, "Who are you?" You'd want to know the identity of anyone who would make such a request.

The blessed Spirit wants to do that very thing, to come in and live in us for the rest of our lives. So we have a perfect right to ask Him for His spiritual Visa, MasterCard, Social Security card, driver's license, and any other identification He might have.

If He is going to enjoy an even closer intimacy than we share with our loved ones, it is time to let the "wind" (if I may use the expression) blow away the foggy mists of uncertainty. First, He is not a ghost in the current, popular usage of the word. When I was a little boy, all kinds of ghosts floated around in my mind. Halloween was the time when they all came out of hiding and walked, or maybe I should say floated, down the streets of our town. I was a mass of inner contradictions. I wanted to see one, and yet when I saw someone running down the street with a white sheet over himself on Halloween, it scared me. I sometimes had bad dreams about ghosts.

So when we went to church on Sunday morning and stood up and said, "I believe in the Holy Ghost," I had an image of a white-robed somebody running through the streets on Halloween. This image didn't exactly create a worshipful attitude within me.

Even after I was grown, it was difficult for me to shake these images. Obviously, it is the same for others, too. I have a friend who was filled with the

Holy Spirit, and some of his skeptical acquaintances nicknamed him Spook!

I realize that the King James Version of the Scriptures is precious to a lot of people (and to me also). However, I would not be honest if I didn't say that I was greatly relieved to find that most contemporary translations speak of the Holy Spirit.

Still, I think I can assure you that He will not be offended if you speak of Him as the blessed Holy Ghost.

So Who Is He?

The Bible introduces the Holy Spirit to humankind. The Bible is His résumé: who He is, where He came from when He visited the earth, what He is doing, and what He proposes to do. It's all there.

He is the third person of the Trinity. Jesus affirmed the truth of the Trinity in the Great Commission. He said, "Go therefore and make disciples of all the nations, baptizing them in the name of the Father and of the Son and of the Holy Spirit" (Matt. 28:19).

Jesus told the Samaritan woman at Jacob's well that He is "the gift of God" (John 4:10). He is "the Promise of the Father" (Acts 1:4).

Are God the Father, the Son, and the Holy Spirit the Same?

Yes, they are! Absolutely, positively, and unequivocally. We are not speaking of three different gods. This is why we said that if we are afraid of the Holy Spirit in our lives or church, we are actually afraid of God!

Perhaps you are asking, "But how can this be? One could not be Charles Lindbergh, Babe Ruth, and Dwight Eisenhower at the same time, so how can God be three persons simultaneously?" I do not have an answer to that, except to say that this question attempts to impose our human limitations on God. It is as if our pet puppy should think, observing a human with its little puppy mind, "I can't speak aloud, drive a car, or hit a golf ball, so if I can't do it, how can you?" The puppy would be imposing its limitations on us.

This does not mean that God has asked that we avoid examining this or any other matter. We are to love Him with our minds; however, I must honestly say that it ultimately takes more than just intellectual ability to believe this.

Without meaning to sound arrogant, self-righteous, or superior, I would like simply and humbly to say that I know in my spirit that the Trinity is one God in three persons. I know it in four different ways, no one of which answers all my questions but, when added together, more than convince me. How do I know it? I know it by logic, illustration, God's Word, and faith.

I Know It by Logic

The highest form of truth must always be expressed in seemingly contradictory terms, in other words, in paradox. You can say, "Iron cannot float," and that is apparent truth. But a higher form of truth tells us, "True, but ships are made of iron, and they float." That is a seeming contradiction.

Again, we know that any object that is heavier

than air, when thrown into the air, must come down. Everyone knows that is truth because of the laws of gravity. But it is only apparent truth. For we also know that metal airplanes are heavier than air. Yet they fly because of certain higher laws of lift and thrust. These laws have taught us that objects heavier than air do not always have to fall to the ground immediately. We call it flying.

The Trinity is certainly the highest form of truth, for there is no higher law than the almighty God. He is the designer and the engineer of all the laws that operate in the universe.

So logic tells me that God, Jesus Christ, and the Holy Spirit can be and are one and the same God. It tells me that the Trinity is an expression and an illustration of a higher law that has not yet been revealed to us. It also tells me that this can be expressed only in human terms that are seemingly contradictory.

I Know It by Illustration

Most communicators know that all illustrations break down if carried too far. But illustrations add to the certainty of the total evidence. When we cannot explain, we can only illustrate.

So how can God, Jesus, and the Holy Spirit be one and the same? We cannot yet explain it, but we can illustrate it. The old hymn states the paradox perfectly: "God in three Persons, blessed Trinity."

Here is an illustration to support that truth. Suppose I came into your group to review this book. When I entered the room, those in the group would receive a recognition signal from the cognitive part of their brains. As I entered, the signal given them would be "author."

Suppose my wife, Miss Martha, and our son, Ken, were there also. When I entered the room, Miss Martha's recognition signal would certainly not be "author"; it would be "husband." And in Ken's mind neither of those two signals would appear but instead a third, "father."

Well, who am I? Three different persons? No, I am one person. But to that group I would be revealed in a trinitarian manner—three different aspects of one personhood.

Here is an oldie: ice, snow, and water. Are these three different elements? No, they are one substance, water, in three forms.

The same is true of the incarnation. "The Word became flesh" (John 1:14). Jesus Christ was the highest form of truth, so He Himself was a paradox. He was completely man and completely God. Both at the same time? Yes, certainly. He was not God who came down, slipped into the body of a carpenter of Nazareth, and went around the earth masquerading for thirty-three years. This was probably the earliest heresy the early church had to fight. He was a human being exactly as I am a human being. He slept, ate, laughed, wept, got tired, became angry, and prayed to the Father. I do these things, too. He was as I am.

But then He appeared on the other side of some mystical line and controlled fig trees and storms, walked on water, and turned water into wine. He said things like "He who has seen Me has seen the Father" (John 14:9); "No one comes to the Father except through Me" (14:6); and "I am the resurrection and the life. He who believes in Me, though he may die, he shall live. And whoever lives and believes in Me shall never die" (11:25–26).

What mere mortal would say things like that? During that wonderful week we had with E. Stanley Jones, one morning he was teaching about the virgin birth and said, "I don't believe in Jesus Christ because of the virgin birth. I believe in the virgin birth because of Jesus Christ." Then he went on, "It's easy, for the likeness and the unlikeness I see in His life, I also see in His birth. He's like me, born of a woman. But He's unlike me, *born of the Spirit!*"

That same sort of seeming contradiction is why we can joyfully worship by singing, "God in three Persons, blessed Trinity."

I Know It by the Revelation in the Bible

As we have noted, in the Scriptures and especially in John's Gospel Jesus fully laid out the Holy Spirit's work, stating that the Holy Spirit would witness of Him and glorify Him.

The other day I was grazing in the green pasture of God's Word and found another diamond of scriptural verification. John 17 is sometimes called the other Lord's Prayer. Praying for all His disciples (then and now), He petitions, ". . . that they all may be one, *as You, Father, are in Me, and I in You;* that they also may be one in Us . . ." (17:21, italics added).

Over and over the Old Testament promises the coming not only of the Messiah but also of the Holy Spirit. I found one promise this morning, written even before Joel's famous line "I will pour out My Spirit on all flesh" (2:28). Isaiah said, "I will pour My Spirit on your descendants" (44:3).

The Bible further tells us what the Spirit will do when He arrives. Jesus said when the Holy Spirit comes (to indwell them), He will "teach you all things, and bring to your remembrance all things that I said to you" (John 14:26). "He will testify of Me" (15:26). And "He will convict the world of sin, and of righteousness, and of judgment" (16:8). The Lord Jesus Christ was giving us the complete résumé of the Spirit who was to be given, so He further said, "He will guide you into all truth" (16:13) and "He will glorify Me" (16:14).

Now let me show you something that utterly fascinated me when I discovered it. The chief work of the Spirit is to glorify Jesus Christ. We are told that the Spirit will *not* call attention to Himself (see John 16:13).

With your image-making processes you can form a mental picture of what God the Father might look like, although chances are, it will be eminently false. When you try, you usually imagine a bearded old man or a gray mass of ectoplasm swooshing about from planet to planet. But still, you can bring up something on the screen of your mind.

Certainly, you can call up a picture of what you think the man Jesus might have looked like in the flesh. But you cannot call up a picture of the Holy Spirit's countenance in your mind because *He will not allow it.* The closest you can come is to see a dove or a pigeon. I would say those are pretty inaccurate! He did not come to speak of Himself but to glorify Jesus. Isn't that exciting?

Certain extremists want to exalt the Holy Spirit, almost to the exclusion of the Father and the Son. To do so is to act against what the Word plainly says.

If you trust the Word of God as contained in the holy Scriptures, you can believe in a trinitarian God of love because He is present throughout that Book.

I Know It by Faith

You can eliminate faith and still have a religion, but it won't be Christianity. At the end of every question the holy Scriptures might raise, God has left a blank space across which we must leap by faith.

If one morning God decided to drop some tablets from heaven with the answers to all our questions on them, then faith would no longer be necessary. But I can guarantee you that unless He changes His method of operating, He will not do that.

Until then, we are asked to walk by faith and not by sight. I have already pointed out that you do not have to neglect your brain to be a Christian. But you also have to believe your heart.

Sometimes children can illustrate scriptural truths better than the finest theologians can. Once I was conducting a membership class of ten-year-olds. Trying to teach them about faith, I pointed out that God loves us and we can know that He does. I asked, "Does your mother love you?" All heads nodded.

Then I asked, "How do you know she does?" Silence. Then, one at a time, little hands went up, and the children gave the answers you would expect: "She cooks for me." "She buys me clothes." "She takes me places I want to go." "She says her prayers with me at night." On and on they went.

Then I confounded them. "But isn't it possible that your worst enemy could do all these things for you? Isn't it possible that your mother could do all these things for you and still not love you?"

Little heads all nodded in agreement. Then I concluded with, "So how do you know for sure that your mother loves you?"

They all looked puzzled and concerned. Then one little curly-headed girl raised her hand and said, with just a hint of defiance in her voice, "Well, I don't care; I just *know!*"

That's it. There is no answer to contradict that. That is the bottom line of how I know that God is trinitarian by nature. I know not only by logic, illustration, and biblical revelation but also by faith.

By that same faith I know that the Holy Spirit is a real, living Presence in this world because I have met Him! I know Him, and He knows me. We go back a long way together. I am not boasting in myself but in Him, for He sought me, not the other way around.

That is who the Spirit called holy is. I "just know" that He lives in me. He is one "ghost" of whom I am not afraid!

So how do you come to know Him? What does it mean to greet a Holy Guest? What does it mean to receive the Holy Spirit? How can someone receive Him? These are the questions we will consider next.

Chapter 5

What Does It Mean to Receive the Holy Spirit?

Words are such puny vessels for sailing across the vast seas of meaning. The frail little things get caught up in hurricanes, fierce storms, and great tidal waves of controversy and misunderstanding. We can do a much better job of communicating with our eyes, lips, hands, and arms. The first time I saw Miss Martha, she looked at me with her dark brown eyes, and I melted like butter in a hot skillet! She communicated!

But since the majority of us don't enjoy that kind of intimacy with people other than our loved ones, we must try to make do with words. One of my friends recently said to me, "Marge thought I said one thing, and perhaps I did; but I didn't mean what she thought I meant!" It happens all the time.

A long time ago I saw a cartoon that addresses this problem beautifully. Two telephone operators were sitting at a switchboard that was going wild, and one said to the other, "People, people! I get so disgusted with them!"

The other replied, "Yes, so do I; but when you stop to think about it, they're all we've got!"

When we begin to talk about receiving the Holy Spirit, immediately people start hearing a dozen different things. But let's give it a good try anyway.

When one uses the phrase "baptism in [or "of"] the Holy Spirit" in gatherings of people who have not been grounded in its meaning, problems arise. If 200 people are present, at once they form 200 different mental images, and true communication is difficult. For perhaps 150 of them, it is a red-flag phrase because of preconceived ideas, a lack of understanding, or rigid prejudices.

One has a much greater chance of good communication if she uses a phrase such as "the infilling of the Holy Spirit." "Baptism in the Holy Spirit" or a form of it is used only six times in the New Testament, and three of these are repetitions of John the Baptist's announcement. However, terms such as "filled with," "fulfilled," "receive," and "full," referring to the Spirit, are used well over forty times.

How does one receive the Holy Spirit? The Bible is specific in its answer to this question. In Luke 11 Jesus concludes a teaching on giving and receiving with these words: "If you then, being evil, know how to give good gifts to your children, how much more will your heavenly Father give the Holy Spirit to those who ask Him!" (v. 13).

There came a time in your life, as we have already noted, when you needed a Savior. So you asked Jesus Christ to forgive your sins and come into your life. You asked Him to save your spirit for eternity. You received Him as your Savior.

How did you receive Him? *By faith.* We are instructed to follow the same procedure here. We are not to ask for goose bumps, a great wave of warmth, tingling of the spine, or any kind of feeling. We are to ask for the Holy Spirit and receive Him by faith. Feelings, as such, are not mentioned in the Scriptures in regard to Spirit baptism. Many people experience wonderful feelings of joy, but some do not. The gift simply is not given so you can glow in the dark all the time.

You received Christ by faith because you believed the Father's promise. The same is true in receiving the Holy Spirit: you believe what Jesus said in Luke 11:13.

For ten years periodically I received letters from a young preacher friend begging, pleading, and asking me how to receive the Holy Spirit. He was looking for the same kind of experience he had heard that other people had.

But then one day I received a letter from him, overflowing with joy. "I finally discovered how to receive Him," he said. "It was there all the time. I received Him by faith."

I well remember my own experience. One day I, too, received Him by faith. I was surprised when a mountainous wave of feeling did not engulf me. Unconsciously, I had been looking for a feeling. I never saw a shooting star, nor did a laser ray from glory zap me.

It was on Friday, and I thought, "Surely Sunday morning I'll be a veritable firebrand." To tell the truth, that Sunday some members of the congregation thought my message wasn't even up to par.

But the next week things began to happen in me. I had a freedom I had not previously known. Miss Martha received a "new" husband; my children received a "new" father, and they liked him much better than the old one. As the tide rises slowly but inexorably in the sea grasses, by the next Friday I was running over with joy!

Does this mean that from then on I was living on the mountaintop? No, of course not. Anyone who promises you a religious experience that will keep you tiptoeing above the timberline in a bubbly existence, always singing, clapping your hands, and shouting, is not giving you a realistic picture. Perhaps lovingly but unknowingly, such persons are selling escapism. They underestimate the persistence of the enemy.

The Spirit of God may manifest Himself to you in a different way than He did to me, but it makes no difference. There is no magic; there is no formula. You simply receive, believe, and begin to live the Spirit-filled life by faith, and it will happen in you—not because I promised but because He did! After all, the bottom line is that the Promiser is more important than the promise, and the Giver is more important than the gift!

Some people don't see stars or dance around the church. You may, and I truly hope you do; but probably, when you get in traffic the next morning and somebody cuts across six lanes in front of you, you just might possibly pray for him instead of experiencing your usual rapid rise in blood pressure!

I don't know what God may do in you. All I know is that you ask and believe and expect, and God will provide whatever feeling He deems essential at that time. He will respect your personhood, and you will not be embarrassed. Whatever happens, He will keep His promise! Further, He will bless your life with a knowledge of His constant presence. We call it life in the Spirit.

One final suggestion. The day you act on Luke 11:13, write on the flyleaf of your Bible, "On the _____ day of _____, 19____, I asked and received the infilling of the Holy Spirit. Luke 11:13 promised it, and God cannot lie. Therefore, it is settled!"

It is a great frame of reference to show the enemy when he comes against you with doubts.

"A Well of Water Within"

"Receiving the Holy Spirit" can be a misleading phrase if not seen in proper perspective, so let's clear that up. God does not fragment Himself. He doesn't dole out a part of Himself now and a part later. When, by faith, you received Jesus Christ into your heart as Savior, you received all of Him. He did not hold back a part of Himself to be given out at a later date.

The same thing happened to you that happened to the virgin Mary. When the Holy Spirit came, she was willing, yielded, and subservient, and He placed within her the life of Jesus Christ. When you received Jesus Christ as Savior, the Holy Spirit came and wooed you. You became willing, yielded, and subservient, and He placed within you the life of Jesus Christ. He became your "hope of glory," as Paul put it (Col. 1:27).

So, you are asking, "Why, then, must I receive more of Him?" It is not a matter of *more* of Him but *all* of you.

When you were born into the kingdom of God, it was as if the Father came and placed an artesian well within you. In eastern Colorado there are lots of these wells. They don't have to pump the water, for the extreme pressure deep in the earth forces the water up through the pipes 24 hours a day. A great artesian well is placed within you, but a cap is screwed down tightly on the pipe. The cap stands for the lordship of Jesus Christ over all of your life.

Only you can unscrew the cap and release the powerful stream of water within. No preacher can do it for you; the angels won't touch it; and the mere belief in some doctrine will only tighten the cap further. It is always up to you to unscrew the cap. Then the living water begins to flow. It truly is a second blessing!

That is why Jesus said *you* must perform the action. You do it by an act of the will, by simply saying from your heart, in effect, "He promised He would fill me if I asked, and I believe God cannot lie! Father, I now receive Your Spirit." Perhaps someone will lay hands on your head, but you are responsible for receiving. *Spirit* and *wind* are the same word in Hebrew. There is no formularized method, because you cannot formularize the wind. You may receive the Holy Spirit anytime, anyplace you choose.

Then, when He becomes Lord of all of your life— that is, your hands, feet, tongue, eyes, mind, job, and family—you are empty of yourself. He comes and fills up that emptiness with the fullness of Himself. Then the living water flows.

The artesian well is not only good imagery but also scriptural. Recall when Jesus, about to burst with His secret, stood up on the "last day . . . of the feast" and shouted, "If anyone thirsts, let him come to Me and drink [you must do the drinking]. He who believes in Me, as the Scripture has said, out of his heart will flow rivers of living water" (John 7:37– 38). Remember also what He said to the woman at the well? "Whoever drinks of the water that I shall give him will never thirst. But the water that I shall give him will become in him a fountain of water springing up into everlasting life" (John 4:14). Other translations say "a well of water."

A river, a spring, and a well! There's a well in you, waiting to be uncapped!

Here's something even more exciting! Let's read it again. Luke 11:13 says, "If you then, being evil, know how to give good gifts to your children, how much more will your heavenly Father give the Holy Spirit to those who ask Him!" The Greek word for "give" is *didomi*, used twice in this promise. One of its meanings is "to bring forth"! So "if you then, being evil, know how to *bring forth* good gifts to your children, how much more will the heavenly Father *bring forth* the Holy Spirit to those who ask Him!"

At pentecost the well was uncapped, and the Spirit brought forth the living water that was in them but had not been released. And in 120 of them the Jesus who was their Savior became their Lord. We yoke *Savior* and *Lord* together conversationally, but in the infilling the term *Lord* becomes functional. Their Savior also became Lord of their lives. Many, many people profess that Jesus Christ is Lord of their lives. But it is only a term and not a functioning fact. *Lord* means "absolute ruler over all."

A friend of mine tells of a college student who unscrewed the cap from his well and was filled with the Holy Spirit. Someone asked him, "What is the difference in your life?" His answer was, "A year ago Jesus Christ was *resident* in my life. Now he is *president* of my life!"

When Jesus is Lord, He is free to do with our total lives anything and everything He wants to do, including our wills, our vocations, our households, our money, our minds, our hands, our feet, our eyes, our ears, and our tongues. They are all totally His, to do with as He wills. We hold back nothing for ourselves.

When, from our free will and desire, we ask the Father to take over everything, He will, and then we are filled with Him. Paul called it "the fullness of God" (Eph. 3:19). It makes sense. How can we be filled if we are not first emptied?

Is it risky? I used to think so. I would tell Him in prayer, "Father, I have risked everything on you." But one day the Spirit said to me, "If my Word is the only thing in this world that never changes, how can that be risky?"

If you think change is risky, then receiving the Spirit is risky, because when you are truly Spirit-filled, you will definitely be changed. At pentecost the disciples were set free from other spirits by the Holy Spirit. They were changed. It took longer for some than others, I imagine, but they were changed.

They were set free from the spirit of covetousness (best seats in the kingdom), spirits of fear (boldness given), spirits of selfishness (community living), and, I am certain, other spirits as well—perhaps the spirits of such things as jealousy, gossip, and nit-picking.

Some of the change takes place as we grow. One morning a couple of years ago as I was walking and praying, I said, "Lord, if there are any areas of my life that need cleaning out, of which I am unaware, please show me."

It is a dangerous thing to ask if you don't want an answer. The inner Voice said to me, "You have developed a spirit of criticism."

I was horrified. A nice guy like me? Unthinkable! But as I probed and remembered, to my utter horror I found that the Lord knew what He was talking about. Doesn't He always? Unknowingly, I had allowed this spirit to develop. At the drop of a hat I would criticize a pastor, a church, a friend, or the way our children were raising our grandchildren.

I prayed from the depths of my heart, sorrowfully asking His forgiveness. Then I said, "Please, Lord, take this away from me. Give me an image of Your hand placed on my lips the next time I begin to be critical or judgmental!"

He has honored that request. I wish I could tell you that I never criticize now. I'm afraid I'm not perfect yet; but I testify that almost every time I am tempted, I see the image of my Lord's nail-scarred hand on my mouth, and I keep quiet. Try it!

The Necessity of Refilling

We are spirit beings; we have minds; and we live in bodies. Our spirits function much like a fine automobile. Whether it's a Rolls Royce spirit or a compact-car spirit, it must have spiritual gasoline to run. For our spirits to function as they were intended, we need spiritual energy. It is that which the blessed Holy Spirit supplies.

At pentecost (see Acts 2) the apostles were filled with the Spirit, but before long they were refilled. Peter and John, going to the temple to pray, met a man who had been lame from birth. Every day someone carried him to the gate of the temple, where he begged for alms. Peter boldly took him by the hand and proclaimed healing to him in the name of Jesus. To the astonishment of the onlookers, he ran leaping and praising God.

When a crowd gathered, Peter began to preach, but the temple police came and arrested them. After being ordered to cease preaching, they were released the next day and joined their friends for a prayer of thanksgiving together. Then the Bible says,

"When they had prayed, the place where they were assembled together was shaken; and they were all filled with the Holy Spirit, and they spoke the word of God with boldness" (Acts 4:31). The same people who were filled at pentecost were filled again—refilled. There was a once-and-for-allness about the first filling, but they had to be renewed.

We must replenish our spiritual energy from time to time. That is why it is vital for every follower who is sincere to have a few friends who are also Spirit-filled. Spiritual warfare is constant. There are no cease-fire agreements, no off days.

Constancy in knowing God through the Scriptures, through meeting the needs of others, through witnessing (boldly at times), through intercession—these are the elements that keep the channels open for spiritual renewal. Sometimes we need retreats with other seekers, where we can have mountaintop experiences and be refilled.

The Holy Spirit is the refiller. The Greek word for "renewing" is *anakainosis*. It is used only twice in the New Testament, once in Romans 12:2, which speaks of being "transformed by the renewing of your mind." The other reference is Titus 3:5: "through the washing of regeneration and renewing of the Holy Spirit."

So the Spirit is the renewer. The water in the well is always there waiting, but we have control of the cap. In a very real sense, the Spirit-filled life is a filled and refilled life. As with marriage, there is a once-and-for-allness about it, but in a sense, it must be reaffirmed every day. If it isn't, trouble could lie ahead.

Now it's time to apply these teachings about the

Spirit-filled life to Monday-morning, biscuit-and-gravy living, where bosses are crabby, babies cry, rain spoils picnics, and income taxes are due; where there are unanswerable questions; and where heartbreak and calamity, dressed in many different garbs, constantly stalk us.

The Spirit is at His best in the midst of all that! To talk about the Spirit-filled life is easy. But to live it daily is not so easy. Does it work there? That's where it works best!

Chapter 6

What Do You Mean— "A Spirit-Filled Life"?

I want to ask you to chisel this into the marble of your memory in big, bold, Old English lettering and light it up with brilliant, red neon tubing so it will constantly be before you: *No one can live in ecstasy all the time!*

I have indicated this previously, but it needs to be said again and again. Whoever promises you a religious experience in which you skip along, shooting out blue and orange laser beams of bubbly joy is reading something into the Word that simply isn't there.

If you doubt that, I invite you to take a long, serious look at our Lord's life here on earth. He had hardly arrived as a baby before a jealous king issued orders for His death. Almost the very moment He began to preach, He made enemies who infiltrated the crowds and hung around trying to trip Him up in His teaching, hoping He would say something so blasphemous that they could demand the death penalty. They lied about Him, kicked Him out of His hometown, took up stones against Him. Finally, they arrested Him, gave Him a fake trial, dragged Him off to a sandy mountain, and suspended Him from a cross. Heaven forsook Him, and earth wouldn't have Him, so they hung Him halfway between, where He died a lingering death of horror.

I ask you, in all honesty, how can you take the religion of *that* man and make of it some kind of religion that will leave you dancing in the streets twenty-four hours a day?

Does this mean there is no joy in the Spirit-filled life? No, it certainly does not mean that. There is joy, plenty of it. But it's a different kind of joy from the way the world defines it. It is closer to what the world calls peace, but that's indefinable, too, because this kind of peace passes all our understanding! Medicine can't diagnose it; psychology can't analyze it; sociology can't categorize it; and philosophy can't understand it. The reason is simply that the Holy Spirit is the gift of God, coming from the heart of God because He *is* God. Who can define that or understand that? I certainly cannot, but I can participate in it! I can never understand why Miss Martha loves me as deeply as she does. I have never understood it since we first fell in love, but that certainly doesn't keep me from enjoying it! So it is with the Spirit-filled life.

Some people go to meeting after meeting, Bible conference after Bible conference, retreat after retreat. Some are truly seeking more of God, but many are seeking to find some kind of wispy, ideal state in which there will be no more trouble, just shouting and laughter.

The joy the Spirit-filled life brings does not depend on one's circumstances. It does not depend on moods. You and I are creatures of the flesh, and that flesh is mercurial by nature. It is subject to mood levels that constantly change, being subject to rainy days, financial insecurity, sick babies, impatient bosses, grouchy husbands, and teenagers who sometimes build mountains of stress on the smooth plains of their parents' lives. The deep joy of the Spirit-filled life does not depend on circumstances or how one feels. It is always there. Sometimes it is buried so deep among the circumstances that you have to probe to find it, but it is always there.

When the Holy Spirit came into your life, He came in to stay, to abide as long as you wish. We have been promised that He will never leave us or forsake us and that He is always with us.

Paul was filled with the Holy Spirit. When he prayed, the Spirit kicked down the walls of a Philippian jail, and the jailer and his family were born into the kingdom. A snake that was 100 percent fatal in its bite fastened itself to his hand, and he shook it off like a clinging wet leaf. But one day in a Roman jail cell he prayed again, and tradition has it that he was executed. But when the ax hit his neck, the Holy Spirit was just as much with him as in the dark midnight of that jail in Philippi.

Peter was sentenced to die the next day, and the church prayed. An angel came and delivered him from prison. The church prayed again, but tradition has it that he was taken out rejoicing to be crucified upside down at his own request, for he felt unworthy to die as the Savior had.

When Paul and Peter were martyred, the Spirit of God was in them just as fully and powerfully as He was at pentecost or on the dusty road to Damascus.

What Does It Mean to Live It— in Bacon-and-Egg Terms?

I do not know how to answer that question in objective, analytical terms. The only answer I have comes from my own experience in living the Spirit-filled life. Therefore, you must forgive me for the number of times I will refer to myself in this section. Yet when a person says, "I know because this is what happened to me," that person has laid a solid foundation on which someone else can build his faith.

Here is an illustration that explains what it means

to live the Spirit-filled life. Place a pan of water on an electric stove and turn the knob to high. In a few moments it will begin to boil, and if you leave it on high, it will boil furiously. Then turn the knob down to simmer, and in a moment the boiling will cease. The pan of water will sit there and will not appear to be hot at all. But if you stick your finger in it, you will quickly discover that it is very hot!

If you watch that pan of water intently, you will see that from time to time a tiny, almost indiscernible bubble will form at the bottom of the pan. It will break loose and work its way to the top, where it will explode when it reaches the surface. Also, since the water is already hot, if you turn the knob back to high, it almost instantly reaches a boiling point again.

Now let's apply that. There came a moment when I grew tired of knowing and believing the biblical narrative *about* Jesus, when I realized that He wanted to be something more than my Savior. So I invited His Holy Spirit to become Lord and Ruler of all of my life.

There was a moment when I unscrewed the cap to the well within me and set Him free to use every part of my body, mind, and spirit. When I asked the Father for the Holy Spirit and released Him to take command, He did, and by faith I was filled with the Holy Presence because I was emptied of self.

I love it when I'm boiling, but I do not live on boil all the time. I have no desire to boil all the time. If I did, it would make a lot of people around me very uncomfortable. I also know what happens to a pan of water if you go off and leave it boiling. Soon it boils dry.

Most of the time I live my life on simmer. Deep down I am always ready to boil. My glory valve is always on red alert! If you turn me up, I boil pretty easily. A great sermon, a quickening word from the Scriptures, a great worship service, a sunset, glorious autumn leaves, grandchildren running toward me with open arms, visibly answered prayers—these are a few of the things that bring me up to boil quickly. But I don't depend on these things, for they are fleeting and transient. I depend on His Word and His presence, and that ultimately has very little to do with one's feelings and everything to do with one's faith!

Perhaps you have asked the Father for the Holy Spirit, but it is just not your nature to boil. All your life you have said, "I don't display my emotions." I don't know what God will do in you, but here is what He did in me. I was an unemotional person. A tear rarely slipped down my cheek until I was forty-five years of age. Only as a child or at the funeral of someone dear did I ever feel my eyes moisten. But since I began walking with the Spirit, He has changed all of that. As I said, I go from simmer to boil in a moment, and sometimes the tears flow easily and naturally. When the church begins a celebration in hymns and Scripture choruses, many times tears of joy and from the anointing begin to slip down my cheeks. I am never ashamed of them, and I thank God for softening my heart. A tender heart is a precious gift from God and is a beautiful thing in His sight.

I have down days now and then. Are you surprised? Sure I do; I still live in the flesh. I'm no super Christian. I stopped pretending to be that a long time ago. However, those days are rare, and I have noticed, as I grow older, that they're becoming fewer and fewer. That encourages me. If you are a new Christian, I hope it encourages you too.

But even on down days, days when I'm definitely on simmer, I find that sometime during the day a little joy bubble forms way down in the bottom of my heart. It breaks loose and wiggles its way to my lips, and I can say, "Well, glory!"

Secrets of the Spirit-Filled Life

Secret 1: Make Him Your Best Friend

Did you ever stop to think that the Holy Spirit is the only one of the Godhead who is active on earth at this time? The Scriptures tell us that Jesus Christ ascended into heaven and that He will come again from heaven. Hebrews 1 tells us that "when He had by Himself purged our sins, [He] sat down at the right hand of the Majesty on high" (v. 3). But the Holy Spirit at pentecost came to be with us, to live in us, to guide us, and to help us let the life of Christ flow from us.

He is no coach, standing on the sidelines and sending in instructions. He is in the game. He goes with us. The Holy Spirit shatters the brittle glass of loneliness. He frees us from the dark prison of doubt. He throws us the rope of hope when we are trapped in the pit of despair. He energizes faith so that fear is electrocuted and overcoming power flows through our beings. The flag of the great I AM flies over the corner tower of the castle of our lives, proclaiming to us and to the world that He resides within us.

I am so glad that fact is not changed by our feelings. Many times I have heard people say in discouragement, "I just feel my prayers go no higher than the ceiling"—as if the Spirit is out there somewhere floating around, busy raising flowers and tending His garden or perhaps overhauling a whirling planet that has gone astray.

He is with us at *all* times. He will never leave us. He is closer than our latest breath; if we take a step toward Him, we step past Him. The Holy Spirit is our best friend, and we need to cultivate our relationship with Him and get to know Him.

How do we do that? The same way we make earthly friends: by communicating with Him. The Scriptures admonish us to "pray without ceasing" (1 Thess. 5:17). This certainly does not mean to pray nonstop twenty-four hours a day. It means to create a *climate* of prayer around oneself so that many, many times each day we speak to our best Friend and listen for His answers. When it becomes a life-style, eventually prayer will wrap itself around us like a plastic bubble in which we move every hour of the day. Eventually, it will become natural. When we have a moment, we will visit with our best Friend.

Every day has its little paragraph indentions of time when you find yourself alone. So when you drive to work or to the supermarket, you will find yourself in a constant climate of prayer.

After I explained this to someone, she asked, "But what would I say? I'd run out of things after a while."

No problem. When you have nothing else to say, praise Him *from* your spirit and *in* His Spirit. The Spirit loves it when we praise God. The Word tells us, speaking of the Father,

You are holy,
Enthroned in the praises of Israel (Ps. 22:3).

We are the new Israel. He inhabits our praise!

Why is the Spirit pleased when we praise God? Is God so uncertain of Himself that He must constantly have His ego reinforced with adulation? No, God doesn't even have an ego (and I want to stop and praise Him for *that*). He desires our praise because He knows that when we praise Him, His biggest handicaps, ourselves, are out of the way. Helping us get self out of the way is His biggest job in growing us into the likeness of His Son.

Make Him your best Friend and pray constantly.

Secret 2: Find an Earthly Best Friend

We are made for fellowship. We need other people but not just to be in a crowd. Those who constantly need a crowd dread being alone, when they must face themselves. Some people do not dare to be alone.

It is a tremendous job to wear a mask all the time, to pretend, to fake it when we know the garbage inside us and when we know how weak in the flesh we are and how much help we need. So besides the blessed Spirit, we need someone, as the saying goes, "with skin on"—and not just a Christian friend but a deeply committed Christian friend, someone to whom we can pour out our needs, to whom we can dare to make ourselves vulnerable.

How blessed we are to have such a friend. If we have more than one, we are blessed immeasurably. You can make it if you are locked in a prison cell alone for five years, because God will provide the grace. But as a general rule we must have a best friend. If you don't have such a friend, start considering your friends today and choose one relationship to cultivate and develop. That person is probably looking for a best friend too.

Secret 3: Spend Much Time in the Word of God

In the Word God has revealed as much of Himself as we are capable of learning at our present stage of development. So if the Holy Spirit is to be our best Friend, we must learn all we can. In His Word God makes Himself vulnerable to us. He dares to make breathtaking promises that try our faith. He shows that He is so self-confident that He is not intimidated by becoming a baby in a manger. He reveals His protection and His loving care. He demonstrates and assures us of His power. So if we are going to know our best Friend, we must spend time in what He has written for us—even to the point of ignoring our feelings and going to that Word when we don't feel like it.

I promise you that riches upon riches await persons who yearn for God so much that they discipline themselves to constant and regular immersion in the Word. It is spoken of by many as containing "unsearchable riches" for good reasons.

Secret 4: Worship Regularly
with the Body of Christ

This is another chief way the Spirit feeds us so that we remain capable of "simmering and boiling." Worship is the electricity that comes to your stove.

If you turn it off, the water will cool, and it does not take long! The Spirit has given us this instruction in the revelation of Himself: ". . . not forsaking the assembling of ourselves together, . . . but exhorting one another" (Heb. 10:25).

Once someone wrote a letter to the editor of a newspaper: "Dear Sir: After thirty years of church-going I have finally stopped. One day I realized that of the thousands of sermons I have heard through the years, I cannot remember a single one, so why should I waste my time going to church?"

The editor, a very sensitive and wise man, replied, "Dear Reader: After reading your letter, I suddenly realized that I have been married thirty years, and in that time I have eaten thousands of meals that my dear wife has prepared. Now I discover that I can scarcely remember the menu of a single meal she cooked. But I am sixty-nine years old today and a picture of vibrant health. If I had stopped eating my wife's cooking, no doubt I would not be healthy at all. Indeed, I would have died years ago!"

One of the first things the people who received the Holy Spirit at pentecost did was to assemble together to form a community of worshipers and friends, for they remembered that the tongues as of fire had hovered over *each* of them and over *all* of them. So what each of them and all of them had received, they celebrated together. That is what church is about!

There are many other secrets to living the Spirit-filled life. We could not possibly cover them all. But as we walk with our best Friend, as we develop an earthly best friend, as we spend much time in the Word of God, as we worship together, we will be in the mainstream of His will, where He can "guide us into all truth" and teach us more and more as we live it!

Someone has said, "Talkin' it out is the tree, but walkin' it out is the fruit!"

Let's get to walkin'!

Chapter 7

Gifts from the Promiser

Gifts given in true love are like kisses blown across the room to the beloved—given gladly, received joyfully. God is the Lover, and that is how He bestows His gifts on His beloved.

Charlotte Thelen is a dear friend of ours. God has given her a magnificent soprano voice. Big, round, and mellow, it vibrates like the resurrection melodies in the south wind. She is truly filled with the Holy Spirit, and life holds few greater pleasures for her than using her gift to glorify God. Although her gift was natural and was given at birth, she began to cultivate it and practice at an early age, her development culminating with collegiate degrees in music. When Charlotte sings, she gives her gift to the Holy Spirit, and He plays it like a magnificent instrument. People who hear her catch the contagion of His anointing on her. I suppose that many times people have listened and said, "I'd give anything to be able to praise God like that."

It is said so often that it has become commonplace, but that does not diminish the truth that *everyone* is gifted in one way or another. So we glory in the gifts God has given Charlotte, but we rejoice that He has not overlooked us! What kind of heavenly Father would give gifts to a select few and ignore the rest? It would be as if, at a children's party, everyone received favors except one or two. That would be the makings of childhood tragedy.

The Word of God states in 1 Corinthians 12:11, speaking of God's gifts, "One and the same Spirit works all these things, distributing to each one individually as He wills." When most Christians think of gifts, they call to mind something outstanding or spectacular, like the young man with a severe learning disability who at the age of twelve sat down at a piano, having never touched a keyboard, and within a few minutes was playing breathtaking melodies.

We are so quantitatively oriented in our thinking. Everything, in order to be admired, must be the biggest, the best, or the most expensive. But God's bankbook does not show that kind of balance. He will always want to know, "What have you done with the gifts I gave you?"

We have been reminded that the Spirit is the gift Giver as He desires and that nobody is left out. So for purposes of clarification, let's divide gifts from the Spirit into two kinds, native and special.

Native Gifts

I once knew a woman who could bake the best coconut-cream pie in town. If families were in trouble, they could expect a pie. If there was sickness or death, Miss Agnes would surely appear with a pie, the meringue of which was tall, toasted, and as brown as a hickory nut in the autumn. When new neighbors moved in, she would knock on the door, pie in hand, and with a cheery smile would say, "I'm Agnes Dockery from the church down the street. I just wanted to welcome you to our town."

Some persons are naturally gifted as preachers. They have an inborn potential to communicate. But this gift, like any native gift, must be developed, honed, and sharpened until that skill has approached its full potential if the preacher is to be effective.

There is a checkout person at a nearby supermarket who always has a smile. It is not just an ordinary smile, though ordinary smiles are beautiful on anybody's face. But this woman's smile is a gift. And she is a spendthrift. She spends her gift with reckless abandon on everyone who comes through her lane. I know sometimes she must be bone tired, or have a headache, or have personally perplexing circumstances, but still she spends her gift. Everyone knows it is not a professional act that goes with her job; it is real, and the recipients are always blessed.

Some persons despise entertaining at home, while others love it. They have gifts of hospitality. Others have gifts of business ability, athletic ability, or mechanical ability.

When I took an aptitude test in the Air Force, it showed that I had a good ear for music and tone accuracy, so I was classified as a radio operator. The first time I put on the earphones and listened to the international Morse code, it was coming at the rate of only five or six words a minute. But it sounded like two screech owls fighting in a rainspout to me! I thought, *That's one time the test was wrong!* Yet after practicing for three hours a day for four months, I could copy from twenty to twenty-five words a minute and carry on a conversation at the same time. That is not called genius; it is called developing a native gift.

Miss Martha has a servant's heart. She loves to do things for people, not just for family but for anyone in need. Once I was a platform speaker at a great Christian retreat with Chuck Swindoll, a popular Christian writer of our day. His theme for the weekend was servanthood, and he delivered three messages in which he listed twelve qualities of a Christian servant. I tried to measure myself by them. By stretching them a bit, along with a little wishful thinking, I found that I just might possibly qualify for about three of them. But for Miss Martha, it was no contest. She easily qualified for all twelve!

Everyone is endowed with native gifts of the Spirit. Fifty years ago it would have been unthinkable, but in our day we have discovered that some women have inborn gifts to become great doctors, scientists, and executives. You name it, and women can do it!

One of Jesus' most famous parables is the one about the talents. Remember? One fellow had ten, another five, and another only one; but all were accountable to the king. I truly believe that God holds us accountable for using our gifts, no matter how insignificant they may appear to us. One of the chief purposes of the class meetings that John Wesley regularly held was members' accountability for their discipleship, which is another way of saying their accountability for the gifts they had received from the Father.

The Spirit has gifted everyone, pagans included. Some may never discover their gifts, while others may quench them. Con men may pervert their gifts of persuasion and use them to cheat the elderly of their savings. Others may take daily spiritual bubble baths in oceans of self-pity because of personality damage, never discovering the fields of glistening gift diamonds that lie in them. *Everyone* is endowed.

But we are also accountable. I believe God's people are especially accountable. Paul, inspired by the Holy Spirit, has painted a picture for us in 1 Corinthians 3. Verses 10–11 speak of Paul's being commissioned by God to build on what God has given him, that is, the gift of Jesus Christ, the foundation on which all of us must build. Then come these words:

> Now if anyone builds on this foundation with
> gold, silver, precious stones, wood, hay, straw, each
> one's work will become clear; . . . it will be re-
> vealed by fire; and the fire will test each one's
> work, of what sort it is. If anyone's work . . .
> endures, he will receive a reward. If anyone's work
> is burned, he will suffer loss; but he himself will
> be saved (vv. 12–15).

God, through the Spirit, gladly gives us native gifts. No matter what they are, in judging us on that day of accountability for our gifts, He will not care whether we were the president of the bank or swept out the building. It won't matter if we lived in a mansion or a shack on the wrong side of the tracks. It won't matter if we had a Ph.D. and spoke Latin, Hebrew, and Greek or whether we say, "I seen" or "I done" or "I ain't." In the day of reward before the Father the question we will answer will be simply "What have you done with the gifts I gave you?" We are all joyfully gifted by the Father, and we are all accountable.

Finally, we may give ourselves this threefold test to determine if the gift we think we have is one of the native gifts given by the Father through the Spirit:

1. Does it fulfill me when I use it?
2. Does it bless others?
3. Does it bring glory to God?

If we can answer yes to any one or any combination of those questions, we can be certain it is a native gift, and we should be busy using it!

Remember Charlotte's gift and that of the woman at the checkout counter? They are truly native gifts.

They meet the test 100 percent. Check them again, and you'll see why.

Special Gifts

In a sense, this is not an accurate term, for all gifts are from God through the Holy Spirit and are therefore special: "Every good gift and every perfect gift is from above, and comes down from the Father of lights" (James 1:17). At any rate, we will confine special gifts to those listed in the Scriptures.

Some of what follows may seem strange to you if you have had no experience with the special gifts. If you disagree thoroughly with this discussion, I ask you to search the Scriptures with an open mind to discover where you think this writer is in error, for I will readily admit that is always possible.

But I want to make you an offer from the bottom of my heart so that our priority will be what is ultimately more important than who might be right and who might be mistaken. I want to make this offer in the words of John Wesley: "Is thy heart right, as mine is with thine? Dost thou love and serve God? It is enough. I give thee the right hand of fellowship." He did not mean "if you believe as I do." Nor did he mean, "I give you freedom to disbelieve the Scriptures." I am sure he meant, "If you believe God and love is your aim, then I give you my hand." Amen! I give you my hand also.

The special gifts are given as He wills, but the Spirit maintains control of them. They are not manifested at any time the gifted one desires. You could almost say that the Spirit manifests them *situationally* as He desires. In other words, these gifts of the Spirit are not "blank checks" on which we can write at any time we desire.

Sometimes it seems that just when we think these gifts should be manifest, they are not, and sometimes they are manifest at most unusual times and in most unusual situations. But there is no way the possessor can simply press a button and the gifts will manifest themselves. (As we shall see later, this does not include the language of devotion, which the pray-er may appropriate at any time.)

As we know from the Scriptures, Paul laid hands on many persons who were ill, and healing would result. On the island of Malta the ruler of the island was sick with a fever. Paul laid his hands on him and prayed, and the man was healed. Then the Scripture states, "When this was done, the rest of those on the island who had diseases also came and were healed" (Acts 28:9). Yet when his dear friend Trophimus was ill, Paul was unable to heal him and had to leave him, still ill, at Miletus (see 2 Tim. 4:20).

It is obvious that these special gifts remain under the control of the Spirit Himself for whatever reasons He has, and any attempt to force their manifestation is imitative and false. The Holy Spirit is the manifester, and the gifted one is used only as a vehicle and always at the Spirit's pleasure, as He wills.

Several of the gifts we will study are very similar and indeed overlap. Also, I see in the Scriptures and from personal observation that these gifts are *almost* always bestowed on those who are open to them and are willing and eager to receive them.

A highly respected seminary professor, a brilliant Th.D., told us after returning home from the great revival that took place several years ago in Indonesia, "Those simple people were not preconditioned concerning the power of God. They did not place limits on Him and His power. With my own eyes I saw things happen I would not dare speak about in our country."

Could it be if the church in America, generally speaking, had been as faithful in preaching, teaching, healing, and the other gifts as we have been in preaching salvation, help for the oppressed, and succor for the downtrodden, these things would be happening regularly in *every* church rather than in just a few?

In examining the special gifts, we will use the list found in 1 Corinthians 12:8–10. Some of these and others are also listed in Ephesians 4:11 and Romans 12:6–8.

Now let's look at them.

Word of Wisdom

To me this phrase simply means that the Holy Spirit prompts us to say exactly the right words at the right time. This gift is probably manifested far more often than we give the Spirit credit for. It is, like the rest, given situationally and usually after one earnestly prays for wisdom. Since it is a gift that is rarely publicized, many of God's people have been its benefactors without being aware of it. Usually, only the spectacular gifts get our attention, and surely the spectacular happens.

Many years ago I was called to the home of a prominent couple in our community and, to my great surprise, found that they were having severe marital problems. From all outward appearances they were happy, and the community would have been shocked to know. But there was fierce conflict here, and they were strongly considering divorce. I asked to speak to them one at a time. I spoke to the husband alone for two hours and, as far as I could determine, got absolutely nowhere. I repeated the same experience with the wife; likewise, nothing I could say would influence her. Then I called them both together and counseled with them for two more hours, but I got nowhere. It seemed to me that the entire day had been a waste of their time and mine.

Before I left, I asked if we could pray together. Both were very devout Lutherans, so we knelt to pray. Inwardly, I had been pleading with God for wisdom, and as I started to pray, my mind suddenly became blank. I could not think of a place to begin. Then it was as if the Spirit said, "I'll take over here," and I began to pray, of all things, the Lord's Prayer.

I could hear them joining me, for they had been conditioned to do so. When I finished, we rose to our feet, and to my astonishment, they fell into each other's arms, sobbing and asking forgiveness, completely reconciled.

Only the Spirit could know that after a tremendously difficult day of mounting tension this dear Lutheran couple, coming from a devout liturgical background, could be brought to face reality only through the prayer of our Lord.

The word of wisdom was the gift, and the Holy Spirit used it to resolve the conflict after I had long since exhausted my own wisdom and other resources.

Word of Knowledge

This gift is very similar to and overlaps the word of wisdom. The difference between the two is that the knowledge given by the Spirit is strictly for insight and previously unknown information. Like all the special gifts, knowledge can be counterfeited. It is especially easy to do on television because no one can make rebuttals. But in no case are we ever to sit in judgment.

Once at an evangelistic retreat I had finished the message and had invited people to come forward and receive Christ in their hearts by faith. Several had come and enough time had elapsed that I felt it was time to close the service. But then I sensed a check in my spirit, and I began to speak. I felt strictly vehicular as I spoke. The words I spoke could not have come from my mind, for I could not have known about a certain circumstance.

I said, "A man is present who thinks he is resisting the Holy Spirit, but actually, he is not. He is resisting his wife. She has been praying for him to become a Christian for years. She has forced tracts, tapes, and books on him until now he is determined that she is not going to have her way. Actually, he wants to come to the Lord, but he doesn't want to give in to her!"

As I finished, a man on the back row jumped to his feet and came almost running forward and fell to his knees. I knelt with him, and he joyfully received Christ as his Savior.

After the benediction his wife came to me and said tearfully, "Oh, Brother Prater, you were right. I was so anxious for him to know the Lord that for years I've tried to *be* the Holy Spirit. Tonight as I was sitting there praying for him, suddenly I said, 'All right, Lord, I give up. I've prayed for him long enough. I'm taking my hands off him. From now on he's your problem!'" Then she joyfully concluded, "At that very moment you began to speak, and he responded. Thank you so much."

I never answered anyone more honestly in my life than when I replied, "Don't thank me, Ma'am; thank God, for I had nothing to do with it!"

No doubt, some persons often have experiences like this. It does not often happen to me, but when it does, it is always at the prompting of the Spirit, who knows just when it is needed.

Faith

The Bible teaches us that everyone who becomes a disciple of the Lord Jesus Christ is given a measure of faith. We are told to "think of yourself with sober judgment, in accordance with the measure of faith God has given you" (Rom. 12:3 NIV). God, in His grace, would not assign to any of us less faith than we will need. Nobody is shortchanged in this matter of faith. But the problem lies in our developing that measure of faith near or to its full potential. Sadly, most of us never attain that goal.

However, the special gift of faith is an individualized gift that seems to be given to certain persons at certain times. It seems to become manifest with some degree of regularity through those who study and seek it, those who are open to what God can do through it. In such persons situations occur in which faith rises within them, they are stripped of *all* doubt, and the Spirit is set free to minister.

God has been gracious in releasing this gift through me from time to time, not as often as I would like, but I praise Him for His wisdom in this matter. I am certain He always grants it at the right time and under the right circumstances.

Here is an example of how this special gift functions. Once I was praying with a young woman who suffered from a painful back condition. My hands were laid on her head as she knelt when suddenly, the spirit of faith came rushing through me like a prairie fire fanned by strong winds. I *knew* that the Holy Spirit had touched her. I finished my prayer and joyfully said, "Young lady, God has healed you. I know it, and I praise Him for it!" She stood up with the shine of heaven on her face and said, "Praise God, I know it too! I'm healed!" And she was.

Sometimes two gifts operate simultaneously. The book of Acts gives us an example of this occurrence. The apostles, while preaching the gospel at a city named Lystra, came upon a man who was in a sitting position but was unable to walk. The Bible says, "This man heard Paul speaking. Paul, observing him intently and seeing that he had faith to be healed, said with a loud voice, 'Stand up straight on your feet!' And he leaped and walked" (Acts 14:9–10).

Here are two gifts in action, the gift of knowledge and the gift of faith. Paul was given the inner knowledge that this man was open to the Spirit. At the same time, he was given the assurance that he could be healed.

Again, on the island of Malta when the viper

fastened itself to his hand, Paul did not panic, cry for help, or show any sign of anxiety. Why? It's not normal! If a deadly snake bites my hand, I'm going to get help in a hurry! The answer is simple. The night before in a terrible storm at sea an angel of God had stood before Paul and said, "Do not be afraid, Paul; you must be brought before Caesar" (Acts 27:24). So the gift of faith rose in him, for he had the word of the Father that his life would be preserved at least until he reached Rome. No tiny serpent, no matter how deadly, was going to negate what the Father had promised.

Faith is not a formula. It is also not a quantitative weapon we can use against God to force Him to act. Never say to a person, particularly one who is critically ill, "If only you had enough faith, you could be healed." God's gift of faith is simply an *inner certainty* that comes upon one in a specific situation. Please don't ask me to explain how or why it happens as it does. Who knows the mind of God? All I know is that He is a good God and at some point in our thinking we have to back off and simply let Him be God. We're not going to stop Him from that anyhow.

Don't think that only ministers and faith healers have this gift. One night ten years ago we were having testimonies in a worship service. A young man of fifteen, thin and pale, with sunken cheeks, rose to his feet and said, "I have had cystic fibrosis; but lately, God has told me I am healed, and I believe it. By His stripes I am healed." He was referring to Isaiah 53:5. He went on to say that he did not plan to visit his doctor again and that he would no longer need medication. The congregation was rather concerned about that decision and said so privately.

One morning two years later I was sitting in my study and began thinking about that boy. I picked up the telephone and called the church where the incident had taken place. The church secretary answered, and after I identified myself, I asked her if she remembered the incident. She laughed and said, "I sure do. That young man happens to be my nephew!" (I hope you, too, have stopped believing in coincidences.) She went on, "After he testified that night, his parents nearly went out of their minds for a while. But now he is robust, strong, and healthy. You should see those pale cheeks now!"

I am recounting this incident now because yesterday morning, ten years later, I was speaking long distance to the pastor of that church, who had moved on to another assignment, about an upcoming engagement in his church. In the course of the conversation he said, "By the way, do you remember that night in my former church when that young fellow stood up and said he was healed of cystic fibrosis?"

I chuckled and said, "I certainly do!"

"Well," he replied, "He's as healthy as an ox now. He is married and has a fine wife and two lovely children. You should see him!"

Please do not misunderstand. In no way am I suggesting that people abandon their doctors and medicines. There is no way to separate the sacred from the secular. Doctors are not fighting God. They are used as His instruments, whether or not they know it. People have died because of this kind of presumption toward God. I am suggesting that over and above the measure of faith we all should be developing, faith sometimes rises up in people who are open to it, which, because of their inner certainty, will not be denied. When that happens, miracles usually take place.

I do not understand how it happens, but I know it does! It is time we stopped measuring God by what we think He cannot do!

Healing

Remember that *all* gifts come from God through the Holy Spirit and that when they are manifested through us, we are only the vehicles the Spirit uses. *He* is the One who gives words of wisdom and words of knowledge; *He* gives the gift of faith; and *He* is the Healer.

He is the Healer not merely of our bodies but of our emotions as well. Many of God's people have been healed of damaged emotions either at the altar with anointing and prayer or in the offices of Christian psychologists through long sessions of therapy. By either method it is the Spirit who does the healing by gifting these persons, who act as His servants.

We also need to remember that the Holy Spirit has mercy on humanity in general as well as on Christians. He brings an end to plagues and epidemics. Sometimes He simply says to the enemy, "Stop! That's enough!" and millions of persons, Christians and pagans alike, benefit. If that were not so, the plagues of the Middle Ages, the bubonic plague, the black plagues, latter-day flu epidemics, and yellow fever would have wiped humanity from the face of the earth long before now.

We have marvelous antibiotics today, wonderful (but expensive) machines of diagnosis, and great medical centers; but they are all gifts of God and tools of the Healer. Anytime we are healed of cancer or simply a cut on our finger, it is the Lord our God who heals us.

Still, the Bible tells us about a spiritual gift called healing whereby in certain situations the Spirit is poured out through us, and healing of others results. Again, this gift is almost always manifested through persons who are open to it and are willing and expecting to be used by God in this manner. To such persons the anointing with oil and the laying on of hands are perfectly natural because they are mandated by the Scriptures (see James 5:14).

The problem most persons have with this gift is that when they pray for healing, it is for instant healing. If it doesn't happen that way, they conclude that they failed or didn't have enough faith. In every case in the New Testament except one (when the lepers were healed on their way to show themselves to the priest), when Jesus touched people, they were instantly healed. This fact could be discouraging to us unless we remember that Jesus Christ was perfected in faith and as yet we are not.

Further, if God is a good God, who always gives us the best possible answer to our prayers under the circumstances, then we must conclude that instant healing must not be the best possible kind of healing for us, most of the time. If that were not true, it would happen every time we asked. Remember with great faith that He also heals by process over a period of time.

I am not a faith healer. My particular calling is

that of an evangelist-author. However, sometimes I have laid my hands on persons and prayed, and they have been instantly healed. But dozens of times when I have repeated this with other people, their healing was not completed for six weeks or even six months later. Still, to me that healing was just as great a reason for praising God as the instant healings, for I really believe that God is the *only* Healer. Whether He does it instantly or over a period of time is a miracle to me, simply because there is no way we can heal ourselves.

Sometimes the gift of healing may be combined with the gift of faith but not always. From others' lives and from my experience I have learned that sometimes the gift of healing is manifested through us even when we do not experience a great surge of faith.

But the fact remains that often, even in those who are open to this gift, the human result we desire is just not apparent to us. It is just not there. What do we do then? Give up our faith? We are like a doctor who suddenly, for no apparent cause, loses a patient. The autopsy does not uncover the reason. His colleagues agree that his diagnosis and procedures were correct. It is simply beyond his understanding. He did everything he knew.

So you ask him, "What are you going to do now, Doctor? You've failed." I assure you that his answer will be, "I'm going to keep on practicing medicine! I believe in what my training has taught me. Just because I don't understand everything about it is no reason for me to quit believing in the practice of medicine."

It is my heartfelt wish that all of us could mature

enough in this matter to see that death itself is the ultimate healing. No one ever took cancer, or a wheelchair, or a diseased heart into glory. Surely we have not failed when loved ones go on to heaven after we have anointed and prayed for them. Besides, sometimes they want to go on, and when they desire to, the Holy Spirit will not allow us to pray our wills upon them.

For my part, I will continue to praise God when the Spirit works through me or others and persons are instantly or gradually healed. Also, I will continue to praise Him for *whatever* happens, because I have it set in concrete in my heart that He will *always* do what He says He will do, either in ways I understand or in ways I do not. It does not matter.

All who really believe that the Spirit Himself is the Healer and that He is in charge of His creation will have no problem with this precious gift but will be praise-filled when it is manifested through them.

Chapter 8

More About the
Special
Gifts

I am happy that early on I disqualified myself as an expert with all the answers. I am just a bumbling, stumbling pilgrim, and I think I would be safe in assuming that you will say, "Well, so am I!"

What I write does not necessarily give final answers to any questions except those the Scriptures explicitly give. But you may be assured that I am writing honestly from the point I have reached in my pilgrimage, from what I believe the Scriptures say, and from what I absolutely know by faith.

The previous statement is prompted by the appearance of the next special gift Paul listed in 1 Corinthians 12. It is a very difficult gift to define. You cannot lay it out on the dissection table of analysis, cut it open, and come up with perfect understanding about it. As in all areas of following Christ, understanding is never a prerequisite for faith. Understanding can wait; obedience cannot.

Working of Miracles

A miracle is any happening that supersedes the natural laws as we understand them. This gift almost always overlaps other special gifts. Answers to prayer, especially as they relate to healing, qualify as genuine miracles. When such miracles take place, the pray-er is situationally endowed with this special gift, the working of miracles.

My friend Dr. Herb Bowdoin says that the gifts of healing and the working of miracles are in the same *category* but are not *categorically* the same. He further states:

There is only a shade of difference between the two. His [Jesus'] miracles were: walking on the water, changing water into wine, feeding the five thousand with five loaves and two fishes, and raising Lazarus from the dead. Of the 37 miracles, or supernatural acts, He performed, only seven could be listed as miracles; the rest were healings [here we understand how healing and miracles sometimes overlap]. The reason for this was, we believe that Jesus, who loved people, was more concerned for their physical health than He was the satisfaction of their curiosity or even the demonstration of His power.

Working of miracles is not confined to physical healing. Captain Eddie Rickenbacker was adrift in a life raft with another man for about forty-five days. When they ran out of water, they became dehydrated and were tormented with thirst. One day a spot thunderstorm passed very near them. They could see it raining in great sheets, but it obviously was going to pass by. They prayed, and the storm reversed its course and went over them, half filling their raft with fresh water.

Another time, in desperate need of food, Rickenbacker prayed, and a sea gull appeared. After circling, the bird lit on Rickenbacker's head, and he was able to catch it for food. Who could deny that this was a manifestation of the working of miracles through prayer?

But why are many people more impressed with "coincidence" than they are with the Holy Spirit? Why do we think that if we can "explain" a particular miracle, it is not from the Father? Many everyday experiences would qualify as a part of this special gift.

As I have said, I am simply an evangelist-writer who travels around the country spreading the good news of Christ. But I am happy to say that I have been blessed by this gift now and then. Once in a grand service of worship I spoke on forgiveness, and the following year I was invited to speak again in this place. One night after the service a woman approached me and said, "I have to tell you this. A year ago one night you spoke on forgiveness. Somehow God directed that message straight to my heart. I hated my daughter-in-law. I felt that she was not good enough for my son. I interfered with their marriage and caused all kinds of trouble."

She was choking back the tears as she continued: "But the day after you preached that message, my heart was so torn that I went to her and begged her to forgive me for all I had done, and we fell into each other's arms and were gloriously reconciled. I found that I was able to love her far more deeply than I ever thought."

Then she said, "But there's more. Last summer she went to the lake scuba diving. She was inexperienced and got into water that was too deep and drowned."

Now the tears were streaming. "Oh, Brother Prater, what if you hadn't brought that message? What if she had died and I had been left with all that jealousy and hatred in my heart? But oh, you did, and I just want to thank God for it!"

Was that a manifestation of the special gift of miracles, situationally given, even though I was unaware of it at the time? My highest heart tells me that it was, for the Spirit led me that particular night to speak on that theme. Besides, forgiveness is always a miracle, for it is directly opposed to our natural human spirit.

Perhaps more people are given this gift by the Spirit many more times than they recognize. Our daughter, Judy, was going about her work one day when she "happened" to glance at the neighbors' porch and saw their child floating face down in their whirlpool. She quickly retrieved the child and restored its breathing. To some this would be just a happy coincidence. But to me it was a manifestation of the gift of the working of miracles.

There is a once-and-for-allness about the special gifts. They seem to be given most to those who seek them and who are open to them, but sometimes the Holy Spirit does not play by the general rules. He is not a captive to formulas. Sometimes He bestows this gift on people who are not seeking it at the time, and that is His happy privilege. Pray for "Holy Spirit eyes" so you can recognize a miracle when you see it. Especially be on the lookout for the smaller ones. They are all around us almost every day.

Prophecy

This gift was evidently seen very commonly in the Corinthian church. It also occurs in many churches today. Under the insistent prompting of the Holy Spirit, the prophet stands and becomes a vehicle for the Spirit, usually speaking words that edify or lift up the local body. Almost always they are words of encouragement, but in some instances they may be words of admonition. They are never spoken to the body of Christ in harsh condemnation. If they are genuine, they are always spoken in a loving spirit.

This special gift, like the others, may be counterfeited and probably is from time to time. Some people, because of personality damage, need to be recognized. They will rise to their feet almost every Sunday, claiming to have a word from God, but it does not take an I.Q. of 150 to recognize them. They are to be counseled by those in authority.

On rare occasions a person will rise in the midst of a prayer or a sermon. Such a person should be rebuked, for the Holy Spirit is a gentleman. He certainly would not interrupt Himself, and He would never be rude. If two prophets rise to their feet at the same time, one will always yield to the other and never clamor for attention for themselves.

On one occasion many years ago I was in a church in which a certain woman had anger in her heart for the pastor. At a certain point in the service she arose with a "word from the Lord" and proceeded to deliver a scathing diatribe against the church and the pastor. Afterward, she was gently rebuked by some of the elders of the church, as well she should have been. It was obvious to everyone present that the spirit within her was not the Holy Spirit.

Before my personal infilling I was skeptical of this gift, having heard it used only a couple of times. I felt that it violated the way worship should be conducted. But one Sunday, while visiting in another state, I went to worship in another denomination since I was in a strange city. My heart was heavy because I had had a traumatic experience with a friend, who I felt had let me down. That morning someone rose with a prophecy, and the words spoken applied to my situation. They ministered to my need so dramatically and so effectively that it could not have been a coincidence. (Besides, I quit believing in coincidences a long time ago.) I was convinced then, and still am, that it was indeed a word from the Lord for me and, I am sure, for others as well.

I had the same experience in different churches over a period of several years, and each time my spirit bore witness to what was being said. Finally, I was cured of all my skepticism. Today I know in my spirit that prophecy is genuine, a precious and intimate way God speaks to His people and to individuals. I know it from experience and from the Word of God, which defines and promises it.

Prophecy, in the sense used by Old Testament spokesmen to forecast events sometimes centuries in advance (such as the Messiah's coming), had meaning for their immediate situation. It also had meaning for the distant future. The prophets sometimes were oblivious to the long-term meaning of their words, as were the congregations who heard them (see Isa. 7:14 for an example). Today prophecy is almost always for the present and immediate future. We must assume, however, that those called to be prophets today may be giving prophecies of the future without being aware of the particular event, like the prophets of old.

Let me make it clear that the gift of prophecy, like all the other special gifts, *is not just for ministers and leaders*. It is for all on whom God chooses to bestow it.

Discerning of Spirits

The New King James Version of the Bible calls this special gift the "discerning of spirits" (1 Cor. 12:10). Most people call this gift the "gift of discernment." It particularly applies to evil spirits. First John 4:1–5 clearly explains how this gift operates. Put simply, it means that when we are listening to a preacher or a Bible teacher, this gift enables us to discern whether the teaching is from God or from an evil, antichrist spirit operating within the person, of which he may not be aware.

The way to use this gift is to test the spirit (see 1 John 4:1) of the one who is speaking by determining whether the teacher acknowledges that Jesus Christ "has come in the flesh" and therefore whether the person "is of God" (v. 2). John continued, "Every spirit that does not confess that Jesus Christ has come in the flesh is not of God. And this is the spirit of the Antichrist" (v. 3).

What this means in toast-and-jelly terms is that if we hear a gospel that denies that Jesus is the Christ and that only through Him can the world have its sins taken away, then the Holy Spirit will give us what is called a "check in our spirits." Many cults and clever teachers today deny the gospel of Jesus Christ and present their heretical doctrines in "reasonable" terms. This gift allows one to recognize that the teaching is false. John called it "the spirit of the Antichrist." An inner "red light" warns us to beware.

But let me offer a word of caution. Almost all of us have biases about one thing or another, which can also give us a "check." So simply because the teacher says something with which we do not agree does not necessarily mean that the teaching is of the Antichrist. We must know ourselves well enough to distinguish between false teachings and our personal prejudices.

Most disciples of our Lord who know Him "face to face" will hear an "alarm" loud and clear when false doctrines or perverted interpretations of the gospel are heard. Many years ago in a northern state an orphanage burned to the ground, and many children died in the fire. One minister who was in charge of the orphanage was quoted as saying, "We don't understand. It must have been God's will. That's all we can say."

When I read this in the newspaper, I immediately had a check in my spirit, for this kind of thinking presents God as a heartless monster. Jesus taught that it is not the will of the Father that any little ones should perish. The minister's comment perverted the Scriptures as well as the nature of God.

In regard to the ability to discern spirits, it seems natural that the closer one walks with the Spirit and the more one lives in the Word of God, the easier it becomes to sense errors in teaching.

Different Kinds of Tongues

This gift has caused more confusion and division among the people of God than all the others combined. Every gift of the Spirit may be counterfeited by the enemy. He has used this one to divide believers, to encourage ill will, and to promote self-righteousness. I covet understanding for us so that if a person who is a member of a "mainline" church receives this gift, he will not feel that he must automatically gravitate to another denomination. I covet understanding so that such a person will not automatically feel like an outsider.

Not everyone in the Corinthian church was blessed with this gift. The Holy Spirit made this clear when He had Paul write, "Do all speak with tongues?" (1 Cor. 12:30). The inference is plain that they did not.

The mark of real spiritual maturity is *to be able to reject what another person believes without rejecting the person*. That is what our Lord Jesus did. If you think Jesus was wild about the Pharisees, read Matthew 23. I do not believe He even *liked* them. You do not call people "serpents, brood of vipers" (v. 33) if you are fond of them! He may not have liked them, but He certainly *loved* them. And even though He rejected what they did, He never rejected them. From the cross the first cry from His pain-stricken lips was "Father, forgive them, for they do not know what they do" (Luke 23:34).

The phrase *the gift of tongues* is not found in the Bible. Yet it is used constantly by people today. The Bible calls it the gift of *different* or *various* kinds of tongues. That means, obviously, that the Spirit gives more than one kind of tongues.

What are they? Pentecostal tongues are referred to in Acts 2, when 120 spoke in "other tongues" (v. 4), that is, in languages other than their own. People in the crowd heard and understood them in their own languages. According to the Scriptures, people were present from at least twelve different countries. The crowd in the streets was amazed and said, "Are not all these who speak Galileans? . . . We hear them speaking in our own tongues the wonderful works of

God" (vv. 7, 11). Here was Peter, who probably never finished the eighth grade, so to speak, speaking Arabic and the others speaking the languages of Persia, Asia, and other nations. Small wonder people were amazed.

That phenomenon was what is referred to by many today as pentecostal tongues. It seems clear to me that this type (speaking in a foreign language in which one has no training) was considered by the first participants as a part of the *entire* experience of "receiving the Holy Spirit."

If this is true, then Peter verified this by saying, "For they heard them speak with tongues and magnify God. Then Peter answered, 'Can anyone forbid water, that these should not be baptized who have received the Holy Spirit *just as we have?*'" (Acts 10:46–47, italics added). And again, "So God, who knows the heart, acknowledged them by giving them the Holy Spirit, *just as He did to us*" (Acts 15:8, italics added).

Pentecostal tongues is very rare today. I cannot verify it personally, but I have read accounts of occasions when persons stood in public meetings and gave a message in tongues, which someone who was present from another place in the world recognized what was being said in his own language or dialect.

The second type of tongues is Corinthian tongues. This is the type Paul addressed in 1 Corinthians 12; 14. Because a spirit of argumentation and disorderliness had developed in that church, Paul laid down some ground rules.

Sometimes referred to as "public utterance," this gift is similar to the gift of prophecy in that it is a word for the church. When it operates, a prompting by the Holy Spirit arises in the person, almost a compulsion causing one to stand up and speak in a language unknown by the speaker or those present. The Scripture states that this gift is not to be used unless an interpreter is present who can deliver the meaning of the words spoken.

As with the other gifts, this gift is situationally given. If it is genuine, one does not turn on public utterance at will. It happens by the will and the prompting of the Spirit, not of the individual.

Like prophecy, this gift is almost always a word of encouragement or admonition.

The third type of tongues is known as devotional language, sometimes referred to in charismatic circles as the prayer language. It is also used in singing in the Spirit. Paul refers to it as praying in the Spirit, as well.

In his instructions for conducting spiritual warfare he wrote, "Pray in the Spirit at all times" (Eph. 6:18 NRSV). Obviously, he is not speaking of the public-utterance type of tongues.

This type of tongues does not seem to be one of the special gifts. However, it is the same type of tongues-word sounds.

Persons who use this type of prayer language usually receive it when they receive the infilling of the Holy Spirit. Though some disagree, many believe one may also appropriate it by faith later on in private by making the sounds and believing that the Holy Spirit honors this kind of faith (see Rom. 8:26) and rewards it by expressing the proper and needed prayer to the Father for the pray-er. This happens when one has the faith to lay aside all human pride and become willing to sound somewhat ridiculous at first. Indeed, Satan won't miss a chance to tell one that.

Is this scriptural? Not all would agree, but great numbers are convinced that it is. Anyone who lives in the Word knows that the Spirit can speak more than one meaning through a passage. He may even lift it out of its context and apply truth where we need to hear it. Romans 8:26 is one of these passages. Although Paul was not writing specifically of the prayer language, he told us, "Likewise the Spirit helps us in our weakness; for we do not know how to pray as we ought, but that very Spirit intercedes with sighs too deep for words" (NRSV). The New King James Version reads, "with groanings which cannot be uttered [in our own language]."

If this is true, then the Spirit intercedes and prays for us "as we ought," regardless of whether we are praying in our native tongue or in the prayer language. Paul wrote, "I will pray with the spirit, and I will also pray with the understanding [mind]" (1 Cor. 14:15), indicating that one may do both.

A host of people are convinced the devotional language is affirmed by the admonition that "if there is no interpreter, let him keep silent in church, and let him speak to himself and to God" (1 Cor. 14:28).

Believers in devotional language hold that since the Holy Spirit prays to the Father for us, prayer is perfect and is what ought to be said. Further, the enemy cannot understand what the Spirit prays and is thus placed at a disadvantage. This reasoning is based on 1 Corinthians 14:2: "He who speaks in a tongue does not speak to men but to God, for no one understands him; however, in the spirit he speaks mysteries." *In a tongue* refers to both public utterance and the prayer language.

Finally, this type of tongues is the only type that is not given situationally. After the original experience one's prayer language may be employed as one desires.

Interpretation of Tongues

As we have indicated and as is obvious, this gift always follows public utterance. The same type of inner prompting by the Spirit, almost a compulsion, causes the interpreter to arise and allow himself to be used to speak in English the words another has just uttered in tongues.

Like all the rest, this gift may be counterfeited, springing from a person's psychological need to be seen and heard. However, genuineness can fairly easily be ascertained by the listeners. Again, this gift is not to be used by the will of the interpreter but as the Spirit wills.

Always remember that all of these gifts are not given like presents at Christmastime. They are gifts *from* the Spirit and gifts *of* the Spirit. Thus, they cannot be used as the receiver wills (except the prayer language) but as the Spirit wills.

On the basis of this discussion of the special gifts, the question arises, "If all of this is foreign to me and I have not been given any of these special gifts, am I a second-rate Christian?" We will answer that question in the next chapter.

Chapter 9

Some Big Problems the Spirit Must Face with People

Can you determine what an elephant looks like by closing your eyes and holding its tail?

That's the problem an ancient fable of Aesop poses. Several blind men had never seen an elephant. Each touched a part of the animal and then tried to describe it. One touched the tail and said an elephant was like a rope; another touched a leg and said the beast was like a tree; and so on.

Each was partially correct, of course. The moral then points out the folly of receiving a portion of the truth and proclaiming that one has found it all.

Let's immediately answer the question asked at the conclusion of the preceding chapter: "If I have never experienced any of the special gifts, am I a second-rate Christian?" In the Christian faith there are no second-class disciples in the sense that some are the elite and others come from the wrong side of the tracks.

When Dwight D. Eisenhower was elected president of the United States, between the time he was elected and inaugurated he professed Jesus Christ as his Savior and was baptized in a Presbyterian church in Washington, D.C.

On that Sunday several others stood with him in front of the chancel railing to receive holy baptism. Then the pastor of that great church said a wonderful thing: "We are honored today to have the president-elect of the United States to receive baptism, but we are thrilled to have these others also. You see, the ground is level before the cross of Jesus Christ!"

The Bible says that you are to desire these special gifts (see 1 Cor. 14:1), but nowhere does it imply that if you do not receive them, you are less than those who do. The Scripture makes this very plain. First

Corinthians 12, before discussing the special gifts, makes this important point:

> There are diversities of gifts, but the same Spirit. There are differences of ministries, but the same Lord. And there are diversities of activities, but it is the same God who works all in all. But the manifestation of the Spirit is given to each one for the profit of all" (vv. 4–7).

After the discussion of the special gifts in chapter 12, the famous allegory follows in which Paul compared the body of Christ to the human body and outlined very clearly how each part needs the others. He got rather ridiculous to make a point. He said if everybody were an ear, then what would we be without a sense of smell?

Let's carry that absurd figure a bit further and compose a little parable.

Once upon a time almost everybody was an ear. All the ears had a big convention and were having a wonderful time when a nose and a mouth walked in, sat down on the back row, and were very quiet.

But soon the sergeant at arms walked over and said, "You fellows don't look like ears to me. I'm kicking you out."

So the nose and the mouth left. But after a while the convention hall caught fire and destroyed all the ears because no noses were there to smell the smoke and no mouths to warn them the place was on fire!

That's exactly how absurd the Holy Spirit through Paul meant this passage to sound.

Paul further asked, "Do all have gifts of healings?

Do all speak with tongues [meaning public utterance]? Do all interpret?" (1 Cor. 12:30).

To say that everybody must be a clone of everyone else in order for the church to be the church is like saying that all clouds must look exactly alike before it can rain.

Potentially Dangerous Problems for Those Who Profess Filling and Those Who Don't

I am sure we could say without fear of contradiction that a large group of Christians could not care less about going deeper into Christian discipleship. They are not familiar with the Scriptures, and their worship attendance is spasmodic. Many of them never attend and are simply names on the church rolls.

Some time ago I was talking by telephone with a Christian book editor in Oregon, and I asked, "What do you think the biggest problem in the Christian church in America is today?"

He thought for a moment and then said, "Apathy . . . yes, that's it—apathy."

For a couple of days I could not shake that response from my mind. Finally, I looked up the word in the dictionary. I was stunned. Here's how it was defined: "lack of emotion; lack of interest; listless condition; indifference." That is the bottom-line problem the Spirit has. Far too many people who subscribe to the Christian faith are afflicted with apathy.

Perhaps the following problems are really spin-offs of this large one.

Emotion versus No Emotion

On one hand, most Spirit-filled believers enjoy emotional worship in which they have freedom to express themselves in lively Scripture choruses, the clapping of hands and the raising of arms, and the use of a combination of musical instruments. All of these expressions are thoroughly scriptural.

On the other hand are the no-emotion people. If emotion is present, it must be private and felt personally and deeply, never shown. They feel that worship should proceed smoothly, quietly, and reverently.

The outwardly emotional cannot be accused of apathy. For the most part, they are as zealous in their witnessing as in their worship.

At times I love reverent, dignified, deep worship. I am well aware of the fact that mood levels sometimes determine our preferences, but *nothing spectacular ever happens in a church that must always be dignified!* Such a church can easily become bonded with apathy, and apathy rides in the same wagon with lukewarmness. We have it from the holy Word that God does not tolerate lukewarmness: "I will vomit you out of My mouth," He said of the lukewarm church in Laodicea (Rev. 3:16). So apathy and lukewarmness are serious things to the Lord God. He takes them very personally. In modern slang, speaking figuratively, they make Him sick.

On the other side of the coin, the Spirit often has problems with Spirit-filled people who worship with great openness and liberty, for unless guarded carefully, that very worship can become mere Sunday ritual to them rather than springing from the worshiper's heart. Worship can become simply a means to lift one from the routine of everyday life to a level of excitement.

In either case, when *any* form of worship becomes mere routine, it is strange fire to lay on God's altar. It is a big problem for the Spirit, who seeks those who will worship Him in spirit and truth (see John 4:24). When we worship, it must be for real, from the heart.

Conservatives versus Liberals

Group A consists of those who deeply and devoutly believe that the Scriptures mean what they say. They believe in the inerrancy of the Bible. They agree to some figurative speech, such as the amputation of an offending hand, and to allegory in the Word, such as imagery in Daniel and Revelation. But they believe that the miracles and all the other events recorded in the Scriptures actually happened. They believe in the virgin birth, the incarnation, the atoning death on the cross, the bodily resurrection, the coming of the Spirit into the world at pentecost, the Spirit-filled and Spirit-led life, and the return of Jesus Christ. In short, group A would tell you that they believe the Bible is the inspired record of the gradual revelation of God through Jesus Christ, the Lord. They would say, "What the Holy Spirit quickens in my heart in relation to my circumstances, I receive as a direct, personal word from God." They would never say about anything from Genesis to Revelation, "I don't believe that," for that would be presumptive arrogance toward the Spirit who wrote the Word. They receive it all. For what they do not understand, they await the unveiling, whether here or in heaven.

Personally, I believe that the entire Bible is true. I do not believe that it errs, though I do not understand some of it. However, I certainly do not believe that I am incapable of error.

Group A further believes that Jesus Christ is the same yesterday, today, and always and that the Father does not change. Therefore, all the experiences that are promised and were manifested in the early church are viable and available today. God does not withdraw His promises or change His mind. He does not compromise His word to accommodate the present culture. Generally speaking, this is the stance of evangelicals or conservatives.

But group B would say, "I believe that much of the Bible is true in its meanings, but I also believe that many of its stories are sheer tradition and myth. For instance, I do not believe such things as multiplying the loaves and fish or turning the water into wine really happened."

Group B would say that all the miracles that followed the pentecostal event and the launching of the early church, if they are really true, were removed once the church was established and growing. Supernatural events such as speaking in other languages, instant healings, appearances of angels, and Spirit-inspired gifts are no longer God's method or necessary once "the truth" was revealed. Claims for such experiences in modern times, they would say, are either counterfeit or self-persuasion.

Then group B would conclude, "To read too much literal meaning into the Bible would insult the intelligence God gave me. Therefore, it is my right as an intelligent human being to decide what I think is to be taken literally and what is to be taken figuratively and to decide for myself what I believe."

Probably group B, generally speaking, in my observation would constitute the majority of the leadership of the mainline churches. In their teaching *most* mainline seminaries would also agree with group B. Since I have come from mainline traditions, at this point I feel I have the privilege of saying that. I do not mean to criticize, only to analyze.

But let me emphasize again that whatever one's stand on these matters, a mature follower of the lovely Christ might reject a person's beliefs but *never* rejects the person!

If either of these groups looks on the other with contempt, it causes God and the church great problems. It is the same problem Jesus had with the Pharisees and the Sadducees, and it grieves the Spirit of God. God has called us into a contest to see who among us can outpray and outlove the other!

A Closed Mind

People in groups A and B are equally guilty of this attitude. Everyone is living his discipleship on the level of his maturity and present understanding. In maturing Christians this is constantly changing. God sees us all as one sees a forest. Some trees are tall and strong, while others are scrubby. Some are growing fast; some are young and tender. Still, all are trees, and He loves them equally.

With the exception of the basic evangelical beliefs I have stated, I do not believe some of the things I believed ten years ago. I hope ten years from now what I feel is certain now will be upgraded.

It is the closed mind that shuts out everyone else who disagrees. It also shuts out further revelation, and that grieves the Spirit. The Spirit remembers how long and patiently He had to woo some of us before He could enter the closed doors of our hearts for the first time. So when He sees our impatience and intolerance of others, it grieves Him.

A closed mind is a sealed vault, and the Spirit will not violate our freedom by forcing it open. Therefore, no further teaching can take place. It is a granite wall with barbed wire at the top over which the Spirit will not climb. When Paul argued before Felix, the conversation ended with the pagan ruler saying, "Go away for now; when I have a convenient time I will call for you" (Acts 24:25). There is no record that he ever called for Paul again, but at least he left his mind open. For all we know, he may have called for him once more. But had he said, "I don't agree with your views, so I don't want to hear or see you again," we would know for certain what the outcome of that would have been.

Exclusivism

Naturally, I believe the whole Word is true: the necessity of salvation through Christ, the infilling of the Holy Spirit, and the Spirit-filled life. But this does not mean that I am free to treat those of divergent beliefs with contempt. Again, that is the same sin that Jesus hated in the Pharisees, the private-club syndrome.

At a great conference after the evening service three

men approached a friend of mine and whispered an invitation to meet with them in their room. "What is your purpose?" my friend asked. "We're going to tarry until the Holy Spirit comes," they replied.

My friend told me, "Of course, I refused. Why should I tarry for Someone who is already with me?" It was the private-club syndrome in action.

We should make it a policy never to ask another, "Are you filled with the Spirit?" It is a loaded question, giving the enemy an entry into our spirits that results in either exclusivism or self-righteousness. If we are Spirit-filled and our friend is not, we have an opportunity for self-righteousness. Inwardly, we could be tempted to say, "I feel so sorry for you because you don't have what I have. You have missed so very, very much!" And that response is not six inches from that of the publican who thanked God he was not like other men.

If the person you asked says yes, then we have an opportunity to hug one another and go through the door into the clubhouse of exclusivism. There we can feel pity for the rest who do not "have it."

If we are Spirit-filled, we do not have to advertise it to the rest of the world. Enough love will ooze from us that they will know; and besides, we cannot hide it.

In Genesis we read about the pharaoh who was looking for a man to become the administrator of the great plan for Egypt to avoid famine. When he thought of Joseph, he said, "Can we find such a one as this, a man in whom is the Spirit of God?" (41:38). Joseph did not have to tell Pharaoh that He knew the Lord on a one-to-one basis, and neither will we. The world will soon find out.

Privatism

The Spirit has this problem with persons who are concerned only with themselves. This accusation has been beamed at the evangelical wing of the church. I do not really believe it is nearly as justified today as it once might have been. Nevertheless, privatism occurs when one becomes devoted to God only for what one can receive for oneself. One becomes oblivious to the needs of others and has no interest in fighting social injustices. It's called spiritual narcissism.

Early in my life a doctor friend told of being in an ambulance with the wife of a man who had suffered a heart attack. He had been rushed to a hospital and later was being transferred to another city that had better facilities to care for him. My friend said, "All the way down there she kept crying and wringing her hands and saying over and over again, 'Oh, what will happen to me if he dies? Whatever shall I do?' She had no thought for her dying husband, only for herself."

One sentence defines privatism: "All that matters is what is happening with *me!*"

Pushiness

The movement of the Holy Spirit in the church for the past twenty-five years is something that perceptive people simply cannot ignore. But a large number of the body of Christ, mainline churches (again, the tradition from which I have come), have largely ignored it in their general conferences, conventions, and gatherings. Of course, many local congregations have embraced the movement with great enthusiasm.

But it is almost as if many denominational leaders believe that by ignoring the movement, it will not touch them and will go away. Exceptions have been sections of the Roman Catholic Church and their Episcopal brethren.

However, it is here, and it is at flood tide. With every flood a certain amount of driftwood is carried along with it. That seems inevitable. So the movement has carried some problems along with it, and we have briefly discussed some of them. One of the biggest and most threatening problems is pushiness.

A certain minority of persons in all sincerity has made Jesus the true Lord of life and has received the infilling of the Holy Spirit. These persons experienced a genuine confrontation and full surrender, and their ministries have produced some of the special gifts with the fruit of signs and wonders. They found the experience so joyous and so emotionally fulfilling that immediately they want everyone else to have the same experience, and they want them to have it before tomorrow evening at five o'clock! Further, they want them to have it in precisely the same manner they did. They forget that it took years of wooing by the Spirit before they came to Him. They had been disciples for a long time before finally coming to the point that they were willing to listen to Him and let Him take over and baptize them with Himself and with fire. Typically, instead of letting the Holy Spirit work and prepare the ground in the hearts of their friends, they unwittingly begin to try and *be* the Holy Spirit.

So they pass out pamphlets, send tapes to people, and leave books where their husbands or wives will perhaps see and read them. They earnestly pray for their pastor so that he or she might receive the Spirit. In church school they begin to witness to their experience and perhaps teach about it. Although motives are good, the *experience* itself becomes an obsession, and they carry a burden for others to receive the same experience they had. Instead of Jesus, the *experience* quickly becomes the center of their lives. As a result, these good, earnest, Spirit-filled persons fall into the danger zone of becoming three-God persons.

By focusing so intently on the Holy Spirit, they push the Christ of the cross and the open tomb and God the loving Father into the background. The Spirit becomes almost the supreme focus of their lives. This defeats the Father's purpose when He sent the Holy Spirit: to exalt His only Son, Jesus, the Christ.

Finally, every one of these problems the Holy Spirit may have with us can be avoided if we remember what being filled with the Spirit of God is all about. Perhaps the following illustration will help us remember.

In the Old Testament when a vessel was sanctified by the Lord through the priests, it meant that the vessel was holy for the Lord. It could no longer be used for cooking, washing clothes, or holding water for bathing. It was strictly set aside for God's use. It could be used only for carrying water to the altar or for carrying blood from it. If the vessel could speak, it would not say, "I have God." It would say, "God has me."

Similarly, when we are filled with the Holy Spirit, it means we have been sanctified for His purposes and for His use. We are permitted to say, "I have the Spirit," but that's not nearly as important as saying, "The Spirit has me!"

When the Spirit truly has us, most of the major problems He has with us are over.

Problems People Have with the Holy Spirit

We've been dealing with some problems the Spirit has with us, but we have some problems with Him also. Here is one of them.

Money

When Jesus became Lord of our lives in the infilling, we made Him Lord of our money. Previously, it had been no problem to drop in the offering plate 2 or possibly 3 percent of our income each year. This way we could enjoy the ongoing programs of the church and let others pay most of the bills. But now things are different. Now we find that we have to deal with the problem of our tithes and offerings in a serious manner.

That's what caused trouble for Ananias and Sapphira. Luke wrote in Acts 4—5 that the young, Spirit-filled church was so love-filled that it wanted to give *all* of its means to the Lord. However, Ananias and Sapphira sold some land and figured out how they could give just a portion of it to the church and lay up a neat little nest egg for themselves.

But God would not stand for it, and He blew them away! Aren't we glad He does not deal like that with church members who withhold their tithes from Him today? If He did, He would wipe out the majority of the body of Christ in this country!

The Bible

When the Spirit fills us, we find that we have a big problem with the Bible. Before, we could treat it as we pleased. We could let it gather dust or read a verse now and then. But now this problem arises: what shall I do with the Word?

But this is a problem we can handle. We can handle it because we discover that we are now drawn to the Word of God. We want to read it. At first, it is almost compulsive. The more we feed on it, the more we want.

It was my experience that after my first binge with the Word, this compulsion died down somewhat but never to the level of casual indifference that existed before. The fire for the Word has never gone out! It often flares up to white-hot heat because of a single worship service, a single verse, or a grand message of revelation from the pulpit.

We are creatures of flesh and of varying mood levels. We need not take a guilt trip because we're not ravenous for the Word every day. But I have found that I am always hungry enough for some of it. Then from time to time I go on a binge that lasts for weeks!

Here's another curious thing I have noticed. The closer I walk with the Spirit, the more frequently the binges occur! Yes, after we have met its divine Author, we definitely have a problem with the Word that we never had before.

If the Holy Spirit movement had not accomplished

anything else, the body of Christ would owe it a great debt for calling it back to the Word!

Your Native Gifts

When we come into the fullness of the Lord, we have a problem with our native gifts. If we have the gift of singing, teaching, hospitality, service, cooking, sewing, or administration, we have a problem. For when we are filled, the Spirit asks us to make a ministry out of it. He will give us Holy Spirit eyes to see that our native gifts, if used for Him, can be a ministry.

In every local church are all kinds of people who are hiding their gifts. They are too busy, too caught up in the natural things of the world, and their gifts are relegated to a minor role, perhaps never used or even acknowledged.

But if we are living a Spirit-filled life, those gifts do not gather dust. For the Spirit, who is now in complete control of them, will not allow that.

Think now about your local church. Who walks closest to the Lord? Whose fruits of love are most obvious? It is those who are zealous for the Lord and who are busy giving themselves to the work of His kingdom.

This fact only proves what we have previously stated: that to be Spirit-filled, you don't have to wear a label! Like the brothers of Joseph and his many-colored coat, people can see you from afar.

You could not hide it even if you tried!

Chapter 10

How Does the Holy Spirit Speak to Us?

Alice in Wonderland opens as a little girl sees a talkative rabbit that is racing along in a very big hurry. She is enticed by her own curiosity to follow.

He leads her to a hole in the ground, into which the rabbit jumps and Alice tumbles. Down and down she falls. Upon landing, unhurt, she arises to find she has landed in a completely different, fascinating, and entirely new world to her.

Something like that happened to me when the Holy Spirit spoke to me and finally came flooding into my life. I want to discuss several ways the Spirit speaks to us; but first, in hopes that it might help someone, I would like to tell you about:

How the Holy Spirit Spoke to Me

Right now I am happier with who I am, with where God has put me, and with what He is having me do than I have ever been in my life. But I have not always been able to say that. There was a time when I thought I was the greatest thing ever to happen to the world in general and to my denomination in particular. Practically everything I said, everywhere I went, and everything I did had as its underlying motive my ecclesiastical success. There were things I should have said to people that I did not because they might have damaged my career. There were things I deliberately said to people because I thought they would boost my career. Every committee or board on which I served, every meeting I attended (and believe me, there were lots of them!), every meeting at which I spoke, I intended to make brownie points with the persons I thought could help me in my upward climb.

I was selling my soul to the enemy, and deep in my heart I knew it. But this awareness didn't stop me, because my ambition was greater than my commitment. It is not too much of an exaggeration to say that if the enemy had taken me to the highest mountain and promised me the kingdoms of the world if I would bow down to him, I probably would have done so.

But at the age of forty-five something happened. All of what Wesley called prevenient grace began to bear fruit, and I experienced a sense of great inward dissatisfaction and a lack of fulfillment. My heart became deeply restless because I knew there had to be more to life than the way I was living it.

"In the natural" I had the world by the tail with a downhill pull. I was the pastor of one of our larger churches, and I had a lovely wife and two teenagers who would make any parent proud. But the Holy Spirit had written into my spirit in yellow highlight, using glow-in-the-dark ink, what an incredible phony I was.

One day one of my more influential members told me that one of our members who was a member of Alcoholics Anonymous was celebrating a year of sobriety that night, and he thought it would be nice if I attended the meeting. Since I always did what influential members wanted, I went. There I found a group of people who had shed all their masks and admitted that without the living God, they simply couldn't make it. Moved deeply, I called my AA member friend the next morning and said, "Bill, I picked up a pamphlet at the meeting last night that outlined the twelve steps of AA. They're intriguing.

Do you think they would work in the life of a person who doesn't drink?"

He laughed and said, "Well, they should. We took them from the New Testament!"

I went into my bedroom and told Miss Martha not to disturb me unless there was an emergency. I stayed in there for two days and didn't come out except for meals. In all honesty I was trying to work through those steps. I did fairly well until I came to step number 5: "We admitted to God, to ourselves, and to another human being the exact nature of our wrongs." By this time I was determined to go through with it, so I made a list of every known sin that I had ever committed from childhood up and laid it before God. It took four sheets of legal-sized paper, both sides.

As you might imagine, this was a shattering procedure. When I finally finished and looked over the list, to my amazement I found that most of my wrongs were against my wife and children. They were not gross, socially unacceptable, crude sins. On the surface we had a happy marriage, and the word *divorce* never entered our minds. In the world's eyes everything was just fine. But honesty means honesty, and that demanded deep probing. I found that my sins against them were very subtle indeed. I was overbearing, demanding, critical, impatient, dictatorial, and fiercely intolerant of any family member who disagreed with me. I respected the opinions of neither my wife nor children. There was no way in our family but my way.

When I finished, I was emotionally and physically exhausted. Nevertheless, I called in Miss Martha, told her what I had done, and then read my list to her. It was the most devastating twenty minutes of my life, and when I finished, I was a broken man.

I lifted my head and said, "Darling, can you ever, ever forgive me?"

Quick as a flash she said, "Why, of course I can." And I replied, "But how can you do that? After all I have done, how can you, without any thought or consideration, simply say, 'Of course I can'?"

She placed a hand on each of my shoulders and looked at me tenderly with those beautiful brown eyes and said, "Because I love you. That's how I can do it."

When she said that, I saw past those brown eyes of hers, way past them, two thousand years past them, to a little mountain outside an ancient city on which a dying man hung from a cross. An ugly crowd was gathered about Him, and I heard Him cry into the gathering storm, "Father, forgive them!"

Then for the very first time in my life I saw *grace* and understood what it means! Then a while after that I cried out for the Holy Spirit to come and take over my life, all of it. And when I opened that door, as the Word promises, *He came in*. I saw no vision. There were no shooting stars. He simply came as the Father promised He would, and I lay back and drowned in the peace of God that passes understanding!

It was not long afterward that Miss Martha realized she had a different husband, my children realized they had a different father, and my church found it had a new and different pastor.

Since that time so long ago I have fallen away and failed Him time and time again, but because He is gracious, merciful, and forgiving, He forgives me and fills me all over again. He blesses and anoints and empowers me because now I no longer know Him as a vague doctrinal term but as a *living* Person, the best Friend I have! And that is how, when I unscrewed the cap, the everlasting water came boiling up, and He simply drowned me in it.

At this point I need to make it crystal clear that He is not bound to any single way of filling us. What two windstorms are alike? He may not come to you in the same manner He came to me; but when faith rises within you and you ask Him, I promise you— no, He promises you—*He will come.*

He stills speaks to me, almost daily, in several different ways. I'm certain that many of you hear Him also. Let's examine some of those ways.

The Inner Voice

The Spirit does not seem to speak to everyone in this way. I have spoken to others about it, and those who hear the inner voice seem to have an experience similar to my own. It is not an audible voice that could be recorded on tape, not a voice one hears through the physical ear. It is a voice in the mind that originates in the heart. The mind is simply the vehicle that delivers it.

I realize that it is possible for us to manufacture such a voice, so I am gravely suspicious of those who constantly say such things as "The Lord told me to wear my brown socks today" or "The Lord said I should have hamburgers for supper tonight." I do not think He is above suggesting a menu for us; but in my own life He usually gives direction, corrects me, or gives me an order or words of encouragement. The

Spirit is not called the Comforter for nothing. He knows that the Christian life is tough in this world, and He loves to encourage us.

How can we be sure it is the Spirit speaking? We cannot always. At least, I cannot. A young Christian once asked a friend how he knew for sure it was God's voice. He answered, "Can't you tell your mother's voice from any other?" "Yes, of course," said the young man. "Well, I know His voice just like that," the friend said.

But not all of us are that spiritually mature, and sometimes we can miss it. One test I have found is that if what you hear is *unexpected*, it is probably the Spirit. Usually, it is short and to the point so you will not misunderstand.

Or He may just be sending you to obedience school. Once the Spirit impressed me in no uncertain terms to go to a nursing home and see an old family friend. Because she was afflicted with Alzheimer's disease and did not recognize anybody, I argued a bit; but eventually, I went. Once the Holy Spirit gets on your back, the only way to get Him off is to do what He says. I had learned that, so I went.

Of course, the woman did not recognize me, nor could she carry on a conversation. But still, I stayed a few minutes. When I left, I felt a deep peace within. Perhaps someday I'll learn why I was to go, perhaps not. It does not matter. Obedience is what matters. Explanations can wait; obedience cannot.

If we live by the inner voice, we will have to be willing to make mistakes. A radio evangelist was cutting wood one day and thought the Spirit told him to go and see a certain neighbor who lived ten miles away. He thought the Spirit told him the neighbor was almost ready to make a profession of faith in Christ. He stopped work and drove to the neighbor's house, but the man's wife met him at the door and said, "Why, he's been gone to California for two weeks!"

But we are not always mistaken. A woman who belonged to our church had been rather antagonistic toward me, to put it mildly, and one morning the Holy Spirit impressed on me the conviction that I should go see her that afternoon. I wasn't too thrilled about this turn of events, but I went.

When she greeted me at the door, she said, "I was hoping you'd come today." For some reason her heart was softened that day, and she began to pour it out to me. She was a widow and had one son, who lived in a distant state. He never wrote; he phoned maybe once a year; and he only sent her a card at Christmas. His neglect and lack of caring were breaking her heart. Like a string of pearls suddenly broken, she spilled out all of that hurt, disappointment, and loneliness. That afternoon I came to understand why sometimes she poured out her inner pain on others. I loved her, prayed with her, and left, knowing that the blessed Spirit ministered to both of us. Shortly afterward, she died of a heart attack, and I conducted her funeral. When we laid her body to rest, I was praising God with all my might that I had obeyed the Spirit that day.

When we feel that the Spirit has spoken to us, we need to obey. If we do, we will be right far more than we are wrong. When Elijah needed God the most, he finally found Him in "a still small voice" (1 Kings 19:12). You will not go too far astray if you listen and obey that voice.

An Inner Conviction

Someone has defined the inner conviction as the "divine ought." We become convinced that we ought or ought not to do something. The Spirit does not speak to everybody through an inner voice. Sometimes He speaks through an inner conviction. This is the way He speaks to Miss Martha. She tells me that she has never heard an inner voice, but I have learned to respect the fact that when she has an inner conviction, it is likely to be the prompting of the Spirit.

One time the higher authorities asked us to move to what they termed a very strategic church. I did not want to go. I heard no inner voice; in fact, I felt pretty definitely that we should stay where we were. Besides, the salary in this "strategic church" was a bit less than ours! Further, it was no promotion at all. This was during the period in my life before the infilling of the Spirit took place. I wanted to climb higher, and it seemed to me this was an offer to step down.

At any rate, we wrestled with the decision for a few days and prayed about it. Actually, Miss Martha prayed about it, and I asked the Lord to confirm what I had already decided: I did not want to go! But one morning she came downstairs to breakfast, and the first words she said were "I think the Holy Spirit wants us to go." I said, "What makes you think that?" She replied, "I just have a deep feeling that's what we ought to do."

Her conviction persisted to the point that I had to respect it, so we moved. Though it was hard on my pride, it proved to be the best thing that could have happened, for it was at this new assignment that I was filled with the Spirit.

One fairly safe measure of whether the inner conviction is of God is its persistence. If it will not go away after a few days, then it is time to step out in faith.

Music

There is more to the story. During this period of uncertainty, while Miss Martha held firmly to her inner conviction, I was in a torment of indecision. You always are when you battle pride and selfish ambition. Those are two pretty tough foes, even for the Spirit. However, although He will not violate our free choices, He knows the way to our hearts.

One Sunday night I was driving to a nearby city to deliver a baccalaureate address. I was in great inner strife and turmoil. Should we move or stay and await that big promotion? To get my mind off the issue, I turned on the car radio, and as the volume swelled, a man with a beautiful baritone voice was singing: "I'd rather have Jesus than silver or gold."

It was the last straw. I pulled over to the shoulder of the road and wept as I admitted to the Lord that Miss Martha was right and I was wrong. After that, peace came. It always does when one is obedient.

In that decision the Spirit very plainly spoke to us in two different ways—to her through an inner conviction and to me through music.

Only eternity will tell how many stubborn, resisting hearts have been melted to surrender by the Holy Spirit when the people rose and sang "Just As I Am." Or whose heart is so stony and stubborn that it can remain untouched when we sing "How Great Thou Art"? Great numbers of hymns move masses and free the Holy Spirit in the lives of many, hymns like "O for a Thousand Tongues to Sing" and "There Is Power in the Blood," or Scripture choruses like "Thou Art Worthy," "I Exalt Thee," "Holy Ground," and many others.

Yes, the Spirit speaks to us through music.

Affirmation

Recently, I spoke on one of the fruits of the Spirit, patience. Afterward, a woman came up to me, brimming over with joy as she said, "I just finished teaching a lesson in Sunday school on patience. God had to be saying, 'Right on!' to me through your message!"

This is called affirmation or confirmation. The Spirit, through a word or a thought from someone else or through other channels, confirms something about which you may not have been certain.

Once during a week of revival services I came to that night every evangelist dreads—the night when there is no clear leading about which message we should deliver. I agonized all day and prayed much, but no answer came. Finally, about an hour before the services I selected a message titled "Jesus Is Lord." I simply prayed, "Lord, I'm stepping out by faith here. I trust You to bless what I do in Your name."

Just before I stood to speak, a woman with a big, round, glorious contralto voice sang a solo. In the chorus the words repeated, "Jesus is Lord."

I have never heard that song before or since, but that night I *needed* to hear it, and the Spirit confirmed in my heart that He would bless the message. Only those who have felt the blessed relief can know the inner joy that comes when, with eyes and ears of faith, one seizes the divine confirmation!

Preaching

I have left the two most obvious ways by which the Spirit speaks to us until last—through preaching and through the Word. I really do not have to make a case for either. God has chosen to use "the foolishness of preaching" as one of His strongest ways of communicating His will and His heart to people. Many times—in fact, most of the time—the preacher is not aware of the impact of the message.

The Spirit is so wise. He never lets any of us see *all* the fruits of our work for Him. It would be too much for our frail wills to bear, and we would begin taking some of His glory. He lets us see only enough fruit to encourage and affirm us and to keep us going.

One night in Houston, Texas, just a few minutes before the time for the service to begin, the Spirit gripped me so that I was convinced to change my message. I began speaking that night by explaining that I had been led to change my intended message, which must mean that someone surely was present who needed to hear what the Spirit had to say.

Months later I received a letter from a young man who was enrolled in a seminary in Texas, explaining that he had been "riding the fence" about entering the ministry and had almost decided not to do so. But God spoke to him that night in such a strong and definite fashion that he could no longer deny the call. I met him several years later, a fine young pastor, happy in the work God had chosen for him.

It is no coincidence that after the Holy Spirit came crashing onto the human stage at pentecost, the first thing that happened after the wind died down and the tongues as of fire went out was that Simon Peter stood to his feet and launched the church of Jesus Christ through preaching. The Spirit confirmed it that day by adding three thousand souls to the church, and He has used that means ever since.

Yes, the Spirit definitely speaks to us through the preaching of the Word.

The Bible

The Bible, in the hand of God, is the microphone of His public-address system.

For those who, out of free choice, will allow it, the Bible is the Holy Spirit's chief means of speaking to people. So it naturally follows that if His people seldom open it, to that extent He is prohibited from speaking to them.

I have already mentioned that this is one of the great blessings that accompanies the infilling of the Spirit. He gives us a hunger for the Word of God. The more we are in it, the more conversant and acquainted with the Scriptures we are and the more easily and frequently He is able to reveal His truth to us.

The Bible promises that the Spirit will use the written Word to speak to us and to guide us. Jesus said that when the Spirit comes, "He will teach you all things, and bring to your remembrance all things that I said to you" (John 14:26), and "He will guide you into all truth" (16:13).

Two ways He uses the Scriptures are through what I call a body of blessing and a quickening of blessing. Let me explain. If next Sunday morning your pastor should read Psalm 23, I imagine that almost everyone there who really listened would be blessed because this body of Scripture is universally loved. So sometimes the Spirit speaks to us through an entire passage or even an entire book in the Word—nothing specific, just a general blessing of inner peace, joy, and fresh understanding.

But suppose next Sunday as your pastor reads this psalm, a young woman is present, a divorcée whose husband has stopped sending child-support funds, who has no job, and whose apartment rent is soon due. When she hears the opening sentence, "The LORD is my shepherd; / I shall not want," the Spirit quickens those lines, which become a fire of certainty and faith within her, and she somehow *knows* by faith that she has heard from God. He has spoken to her through the Word by quickening it, that is, by bringing it to life in her and making it relevant to her need at that time. It is called in Greek a *rhema*, God speaking to us personally. It is not unusual for the Spirit to speak like that to persons who give Him an opportunity, which leads me to stress again the importance of being a Word person, one who walks so constantly in it that the Spirit has easy access to the mind and heart for guidance and instruction.

On one occasion when I was in the pastorate, I approached a board meeting with considerable dread. Some of the members were proposing something I did not think was right. It was not immoral, but I simply thought their proposal was a mistake. It was not really a big issue but very subtle in its implications, one I thought could become a big issue.

In my flesh I did not wish to oppose the entire board over this matter, which many of them would consider too insignificant with which to bother. They would be surprised that I would say anything at all about it, much less oppose it.

In my spirit, though, I felt that I ought to oppose them. But I wondered if I had the courage to do it. While reading in Galatians 1 that morning, I suddenly came to this question: "Am I now trying to win the approval of men, or of God?" (v. 10 NIV).

When I read that, the Holy Spirit lifted it out of its resting place in the Scriptures, right out of that sun-drenched day when Paul wrote it, and launched it across twenty centuries, took it from its orbit, pushed it downward, and gave it a flaming reentry into my heart.

With this personal word from the Lord, I had no problem that night rising to my feet and explaining my position. I wish I could tell you that they saw it my way, but they did not. However, they were very kind and loving, and our relationships, if anything, were strengthened.

A dear friend gave us a beautiful painting of an open Bible with a light shining over one page and a lamp over the other. It reads, "Thy word is a lamp unto my feet, and a light unto my path" (Ps. 119:105 KJV). That painting hangs in an honored place in our home and means everything to me, and that Book is the chief vehicle by which the Spirit guides you and me through life. It is my joy to look at that painting many times during the day and to allow it to affirm in me the conviction I hold that this verse is true.

By storing the Word in our hearts, we give the Spirit an opportunity to bring it to our remembrance by what some people call supernatural recall, something we would not ordinarily have brought to mind, but the Spirit does it when we need it most.

A missionary who was once imprisoned by the North Koreans hid a tiny New Testament in his cell among his meager possessions. One day the guards found it, took him from his cell, beat him, and kicked him with their hobnailed boots until he lay bloody and panting with exhaustion.

He later testified, "Suddenly, to their astonishment I began to laugh softly with joy, for I discovered that even after all that brutality I could love them." He went on, "As the blows were coming down on me, the Holy Spirit brought to my memory the word I needed to hear: 'You have heard that it was said, "You shall love your neighbor and hate your enemy." But I say to you, love your enemies, bless those who curse you, do good to those who hate you, and pray for those who spitefully use you and persecute you'" (Matt. 5:43–44). He concluded, "They took my Testament from me, but they could not steal the Word, for I had hidden it in my heart!"

What a blessing to hide the Word in one's heart so the Spirit can bring it to mind at precisely the right time.

John Wesley wrote in his journal:

On March 8, 1750, we had a great earthquake as I was preaching. A great cry followed from the women and children. Immediately I called out,

> "Therefore will not we fear, though the earth be removed, and though the mountains be carried into the midst of the sea. . . . The Lord of hosts is with us" (Ps. 46:2, 7 KJV).

He had hidden the Word in his heart, and it came forth at the right time.

Some people, in reverence for God's Word, do not mark the pages of the Scriptures. We should not fear to do this, for we do not worship the Book. That is called bibliolatry. I believe that everyone's personal Bible should be well marked. I assure you that mine is. Recently, in our morning devotions together Miss Martha and I decided to go through the rather lengthy book of Isaiah, this time reading only the passages or sentences we had marked in times past. It was a beautiful experience for us. The marked verses stood out and brought back memories of the times they had spoken to us in various situations.

I have one verse to which I turn many times before I speak. I have noted beside it, "My pulpit verse." It is from Psalm 20:

> Now I know that the LORD saves His anointed;
> He will answer him from His holy heaven
> With the saving strength of His right hand (v. 6).

Almost always, if I have made proper preparation, the Spirit quickens that verse to my spirit with assurance.

Whoever stands on the sidelines and scoffs at the mighty movement of the Holy Spirit in our day will surely have to admit that as a result of it, God's people have been called back to the Bible, to the Scriptures, the chief vehicle by which the divine Lover whispers that love to the listening ears of an eager heart. For that we should be eternally grateful.

Chapter 11

The Proof of the Spirit

> He who loves his brother abides in the light, and
> there is no cause for stumbling in him. But he
> who hates his brother is in darkness and walks in
> darkness, and does not know where he is going,
> because the darkness has blinded his eyes (1 John
> 2:10–11).

Suppose you lived in the mountains and I lived
on the seashore. You had never seen the ocean or a
picture of it and, for that matter, had never heard
that an ocean exists. Then suppose I came to visit
you and during the visit attempted to tell you about
the ocean. No matter how hard I tried or how
graphic my description was, you could never really
know about the ocean until you had seen and walked
or swum in it. First, you would have to wade into it,
listen to the pounding of its waves, ponder its lim-
itless horizons and unthinkable depths, and feel its
restless waves around your feet. The only way you
could ever know about the ocean would be to experience it. Even then you would know only a fraction
of all the ocean is.

Similarly, suppose you have made Jesus the Lord
of every aspect of your life—your family, your job,
every organ of your body, your mind, everything—in
a grand moment of genuine, complete yielding. You
unscrewed the cap from your well and received the
infilling of the Spirit.

Suppose you come to tell me about it, but I know
nothing of the Spirit. To me, the Holy Spirit has
always been a foggy, elusive, unseen essence that is
somehow vaguely related to God—a wispy thing like
a balloon on a string, tied to the Bible and floating
around somewhere. Of course, I would rejoice with

you because of your life-changing experience with the Spirit, but I wouldn't really be impressed until two things happened: first, if your attitudes toward people were so radically altered that no one could deny your experience. If your spirit were so transformed that you became a different person from the one I previously knew, then I would be interested enough to want the fulfillment you seem to have. Second, I too, having seen what He had done in you, from my own free choice, asked the Lord Jesus through the Spirit to become Lord of my life and to fill me, and He did just that.

Then I too would have *personally experienced* the grand relief that comes from getting oneself off one's hands and into His. After I had waded in the ocean of experience and received the infilling by faith, only then would I be able to comprehend what you tried to tell me and describe to me.

What Is the Proof of the Spirit?

As I talk with those in the body of Christ, I often hear these judgmental questions asked: "Is he Spirit-filled?" "Is she Spirit-filled?" "Is your pastor filled with the Spirit?" Just asking these questions implies judgment, exclusivism, and/or self-righteousness.

Here is the way I believe the Lord God Himself would respond to such questions: "Friend, it does not matter to Me how well you have your testimony polished and shined. It does not matter to Me how thrilling and dramatic your infilling was. I'm not really that interested in how many stars you saw, or if you fainted dead away because of the power of the Spirit upon you, or if you spoke in another language, or if you were instantly endowed with the ability to prophesy in the church. That is all gratifying to you, I am sure, and I sincerely rejoice with you in the Spirit's manifestation to you and in you. But there is one thing I want to see and know in you. This is what I am looking for as undeniable proof that the Holy Spirit has done all in you that you claim: *does a loving spirit now flow from you toward others?*"

I know that when one receives the fullness of the Spirit, one is not made instantly perfect in one's performance. If you had false teeth before you were filled, you'll still have them afterward. Your cereal is still going to get soggy; things will still go wrong at work; you will still get caught in the rain with no umbrella; and you will still have to pay your credit-card bill at the end of the month. The Lord God will not surgically remove from our personhood all that is unlovely and unholy. No halo of purity is going to hover above our heads.

But one thing will be drastically different: *the deepest desires of our hearts will be changed.* Our basic motivations will be transformed. Now we will want above all things to be what God wants us to be, to go where He directs, and to obey Him when He speaks. As a result, love will begin to flow from us.

These comments are not intended to downgrade the great emotional experiences with which some of us have been blessed. I have already said that nothing spectacular ever happens in a church (or a person) that must always be dignified. But what the Lord of all wants to see in us after the filling is the change it has brought about in our attitudes toward others. He wants to see how we react when people persecute and revile us; accuse us falsely; spread vicious, false gossip about us; drag us off to crucify us.

In 1 Corinthians 12 our great friend Paul laid down guidelines for the church on dealing with the special gifts. He summed them up in the last few verses by saying, "Seek them; I want you to have them; but don't get hung up on them. If you do, you'll take your eyes off Jesus. Besides, not everyone has the same gifts" (author's paraphrase). In the last verse he wrote, "Earnestly desire the best gifts. And yet I show you a more excellent way" (v. 31). Then follows, in my opinion, the greatest chapter in the Bible on scriptural holiness, the love chapter (chap. 13). He wraps up the discussion in the first verse of chapter 14: "Pursue love."

Remember our saying that when we were born into the kingdom, the same thing happened in us that happened in the virgin Mary? She was submissive, yielded, and willing, and the Spirit came and placed the life of Jesus Christ in her. The Spirit did not place the life of Jesus Christ in Mary's womb to stay there. He placed it there because His ultimate will was that Mary should release the life of Jesus Christ into the world.

Likewise, when you received the infilling of the Holy Spirit, God did not place in us the life of Jesus Christ so He could remain isolated in our hearts and so you could twinkle like a star all the time. He did it so you could ultimately release Him into the world and He could live His life through you. When you were born into the kingdom, Christ came to live in you. But when you were filled with the Spirit, you unscrewed the cap on the well so that, like Mary, you could release Him into the world and His life would flow through you into the lives of other people in service and ministry—ministry to those who love you and those who don't. It's called bearing fruit.

What is His life? *Love* is His life because He *is* love. The Scripture does not say, "God is filled with love," nor does it say, "God is *like* love." First John 4:8 says, "He who does not love does not know God, for God is love."

We Are Not Yet Perfected in Loving

Now a word of comfort to us all. As far as I know, no one is yet perfected in love. Jesus Christ is the only human who was perfected in love. Obviously, God's intention is that ultimately we shall be perfected in it, for He said in Romans 8:29 that we who have been wooed by Him are one day to "be conformed to the image of His Son."

So He says to us through Paul, "Make love *your* aim." Let me tell you about a man whose aim is love because he is filled with the Holy Spirit. His name is Dean Culp. When the present movement of the Holy Spirit began in the late sixties, Dean received the infilling of the Holy Spirit at a time when it was considered by many in his denomination fringe lunacy, fanatical, far right, and strictly fundamentalist. In all of the years I have known him, he has never said to me, "I am filled with the Holy Spirit; I have this special gift or that." But he is one of the kindest, sweetest, gentlest men I have ever known. The love of God flows from him like a lovely fountain. He walks out his faith in his daily life, and everyone knows it.

Someone might be saying, "Well, I do very well

in church, but if Dean had a job like mine in the rough-and-tumble world, maybe he wouldn't do so well." Let me tell you what Dean's job is. He is a labor negotiator with one of the biggest corporations in the country. As the advocate of management, he sits down with hard-core, tough, and sometimes profane labor negotiators, often for days at a time, always in a fierce adversarial relationship. But they don't shake any fruit off his tree and spoil it. Sometimes he must be very firm, but he is always quiet and loving. He has had this job for over twenty years, so he must be doing something right.

I called him the other night to ask if I could write about him in these pages. He said, "Of course," and then I said, "Dean, you have got to be walking close to the Holy Spirit to have served and witnessed for as long as you have." And he answered, "If it weren't for the Holy Spirit, I simply could not do it!" Love is the aim of Dean Culp's life, and he pursues it. The Spirit has asked us to make it ours.

What Would Happen If We Were All Filled with Love?

It is a tantalizing, fascinating question. For if we were all perfected in love now, as was the Lord Jesus Christ, here are some of the things that would disappear.

Among God's people there would be no more church quarrels or splits, no more destructive criticism, no intraoffice pockets of jealousy, no hurt feelings or ill will, no divorces.

Gone would be racism, cheating on income taxes, drugs, crime, prostitution, defrauding people in business, unforgiveness, manipulation, mask wearing, and self-righteousness.

Scornful labels would vanish, as would "what if" imaginings and fears springing from insecure feelings. There would be no more doubting of God's Word, no more drunkenness, and no overindulgence in anything. I don't know how long the list would grow if we extended it to its limit. If all these things were manifested in us, we would have attained perfect holiness, as God is holy.

Jesus knew who He was. He settled that in the wilderness before He ever began His ministry. And the Christian faith promises that because of Calvary, when we are born into the kingdom, in God's eyes we are made perfectly righteous, even as Christ was righteous. When we learn and have settled in our hearts who *we* are in Christ, we will ask the Spirit to fill us and take charge. Then love that is like His will be our aim in our daily, earthly performances, and it will begin to flow from us—perhaps slowly at first, but it will flow.

Simply because we fall far short of perfect love, we should not be discouraged. A little sprout does not stop growing simply because it is not yet a full-grown tree. It continues to grow because it has underneath it in the earth the life-giving power to push it to its ultimate destiny, which is to become a full-grown tree. So let us continue to climb upward!

After Growth, the Fruit!

A few years ago there was a terrible freeze in Florida. Many orange groves were destroyed. Some of the growers replanted tiny trees. This year I noticed that most of those trees, now only three or four feet tall, have started bearing oranges. They did not wait until they were full-grown trees to begin.

When Paul listed the fruit of the Spirit, which is the tangible evidence that the life of Jesus is being lived through us by the indwelling Spirit, he listed nine varieties: love, joy, peace, longsuffering, kindness, goodness, faithfulness, gentleness, and self-control (see Gal. 5:22–23). Remember, it's called the fruit of *the Spirit*. *He* produces the fruit. We don't. But *the* fruit of the Spirit is love. It is listed first, the one from which the others spring. Love is the one undeniable proof that one is filled with the Spirit. Show me love like God's love, and I will know who lives in you and who produced it.

God planned all of this very wisely so we cannot see fruit in ourselves. An orange tree does not produce oranges so it can consume them itself. Imagine how ridiculous an orange tree would look with hands and a big mouth so that when the fruit was ripe, it could pick the oranges and stuff them greedily into its own mouth! The fruit of the Spirit, when it is grown in us, is always meant to be consumed by others.

Have you ever seen love in another person that is like God's love? I see and rejoice in it frequently. The kingdom of God on earth in the church contains many large spiritual orange trees, trees like Dean Culp. They are growing rapidly, for they are filled with inner power from which they draw the water and the nutrients necessary to produce the fruit.

I saw it in my own family in my youth. I saw it one Thanksgiving night when I came home hurt, dejected, and in dread, for that afternoon in the annual high-school football game with our most bitter rival I had personally been responsible for losing the game. My fumble at a critical moment lost the game. Darkness had fallen by the time I arrived home. Oh, how I dreaded to go in. I had failed my town, my team, and my family by my clumsiness and ineptness.

But when I went in, the table was set, and the family was seated for the traditional Thanksgiving dinner and celebration. My two brothers, sister, father, and mother greeted me joyfully, and the celebration began. Nobody said, "Aren't you ashamed of yourself?" No one said, "Arnold, that was a terrible thing you did." Not one word about my failure, about how I had let them all down, not one word of condemnation. They just accepted me into the circle of love.

When I was grown and looked back on that experience, I realized that I was accepted and loved, not because of what I did or failed to do but because of *who I was.* And I thought, *That is how God loves me, and that is why He loves me: because of who I am in Christ Jesus.* Love like my family's love that day can flow only from the Spirit abiding within.

My senior year in college came in the heart of the Great Depression. We did not have the money for the first quarter's tuition. It seems hard to believe today, but tuition for a quarter at Northeast Missouri State was only twenty dollars—and that included books! Father did not have twenty dollars. But he said, "Don't worry, Son. We'll go to the bank, and I'll sign your note with you. We'll get the money."

We went to the bank the next morning. The

banker, a member of our church, had tears in his eyes as he shook his head. The directors had instructed him that without collateral there were to be no loans and there were to be no exceptions. We went to private individuals in the community who were known to lend money, but everywhere it was the same: no collateral, no loan.

There seemed to be no way I could go to college that year. But the day before I was supposed to leave, a big truck backed up to our house, and two men laid down some boards from the truck bed to the front porch. I wasn't there that afternoon, but afterward I heard what happened.

There was one thing Mother loved more than anything in the world, besides her family and Jesus, and that was her Gulbranson piano. It was the only decent piece of furniture we had. But the men rolled it out of the house, onto the boards, and into the truck. The driver reached into the pocket of his overalls, pulled out some bills, and handed mother a twenty, a ten, and a five.

Then they got into the truck and drove off with the pride of Mother's life. Father threw his arms around her, and she cried and cried. That night Mother couldn't even talk about it, so Father told me, "Son, you can go on back to college tomorrow. Your mother sold her piano." Then he handed me the money.

Afterward I thought, *That's love like God's love.* The most precious possession He had was His only Son, and yet He gave Him up to be disgraced and crucified by the world so that we could have life, so that we could enroll in His everlasting school to learn how to love like that!

When people tell you they have been filled with the Spirit, their performance will certainly not be made instantly perfect. But if it is genuine, here and there, now and then, at certain times, love like God's love will begin to flow from them into a situation. You will see it, and you will know. You see, love can never be proved by the mere saying of it. Love can be proved only by the doing!

Of the three Greek words for love only two forms of one of those three words are used in the New Testament to describe God's love. They are *agape* and *agapao*. *Agape* is the noun, love identified. *Agapao* is the verb, love in action. John 3:16 uses *agapao*, love in action. That is why that pain-filled cross out there on that God-forsaken hill is love in action. That huge stone rolled away from the tomb in the garden is *agapao*. The swirling, roaring wind that filled the room at pentecost is love in action.

Jesus boiled down love that is like God's love in a pan of truth, and the residue in the bottom of the pan came out like this: "Why do you call Me 'Lord, Lord,' and not do the things which I say?" (Luke 6:46). It is *agapao* that pleases the Master.

The orange that passersby will see hanging from your tree is called love. But the orange will have been borne in vain unless it is given for someone else's consumption. They will know for sure that we have received and are full of the Holy Spirit and that the life of Christ is being lived out in us, not merely by our gifts, either natural or special, but by the Christlike love they see flowing from us from time to time.

I once heard a preacher tell the story of Mister John, a great, compassionate man who was a beloved principal in a public school for many years. He was a devout member of a church and was filled with the Holy Spirit of God. There came the inevitable time when he was forced to retire. They gave him a big farewell party, made nice speeches, and gave him gifts. His pension checks started arriving, and they thought Mister John would take it easy now.

But they did not realize that love like God's love doesn't know how to take it easy. So he went into the ghettos of the city to a soup kitchen and volunteered to work there. Every day he would get into his old car and drive from his pleasant apartment in the suburbs into the teeming misery of the ghetto.

One evening, just as it was growing dark, he walked from the building to his car and was unlocking it when a teenager grabbed his neck, seized his billfold, and tried to run with it. Mister John instinctively held on, and there was a struggle. He was knocked to the ground, while the youth fell backward into the car window, which shattered.

The youth began to run down the street with the billfold, blood dripping from his arm, leaving a red trail on the pavement. Mister John raised himself on one elbow and cried, "Come back! Come back! You're bleeding, and I want to help you! Let me help you!"

Most of us are not yet that far along, but he walked so close to his Lord and was so filled with Him that when it was time to love like God, the words involuntarily rolled out. Love in action.

At Calvary we desecrated His holiness by our sinful hearts, and yet He cried from His Spirit, "You're hurt! You're hurt! I want to help you!"

When I heard this story, my heart leapt within

me, and I prayed, "Lord, make me like that. Let me be able to love like that!" The proof of the fullness of the Spirit within is the manifestation of love like God's love. For that is the fruit the Spirit bears.

What a challenge that is to the body of Christ in this country! What if all of the ordained ministers, lay pastors, elders, deacons, bishops, seminary professors, and every leader in our local churches came together in a great convention somewhere? What if they came, not to caucus and decide policies and programs or to revise portions of their church laws, but simply to seek God's face? What if they laid aside all their political ambitions, their power struggles, and their career concerns and made themselves completely vulnerable by seeking God together until they were finally all of one accord? What if all of them yielded themselves to one mighty week of prayer together, then made a full and complete surrender to the lordship of Jesus Christ over every area of their lives, asking the Holy Spirit to come in and fill or refill them?

Is that just starry-eyed idealism and jousting at windmills? I don't think so. In my heart of hearts I believe if that happened, the Holy Spirit would come in such might, power, and glory that pentecost, or something greater, *far greater*, would happen again. I believe it would not be long until the entire world would be shaken by what happened at such a gathering.

In the face of that kind of infilling, Jesus Christ would be exalted in the way love that is like God's love always exalts Him. True to His Word, He would begin to draw all people to Him. Then the greatest revival the world has ever seen would begin. Such a fire storm of love would break out that the angels would rush to the parapets of heaven and gaze down on the scene in awe and amazement as they watched the consuming fire of God make its way around the world.

Could it really happen? I believe it could. I, for one, am not willing to limit God by saying that it could not. Let us live in prayerful hope and expectation, for we know that faith is the answer but that love is the key!

Even so, come, Holy Spirit. Come quickly! Amen.